BITE-SIZED ROMANCE

A COMPLETE GUIDE TO WRITING, EDITING, AND PUBLISHING CLEAN SHORT FICTION

SARAH LAMB

Contents

This book is dedicated to all who have ever wanted to bring their stories to life.
You've got this.
Don't give up your dream.

INTRODUCTION

Welcome to Bite-Sized Romance! I'm really excited you are here. While I don't claim to be an expert in *all the things*, I do know about *a lot of things*. And I have crammed this book full of information for you, from what to think about before you start writing to what to do once your book is finished.

What sets this writing book apart from others?

First off, I want it to feel like a chat with that helpful friend you go to when you need help. A book that's written in a conversational tone, not one that will make you feel frustrated or overwhelmed or confused with data and charts and words that make you pull out a dictionary.

Been there, read those; didn't like it myself.

Next, I'm not just an author, I'm also a book editor. I've been helping others bring their stories to life for well over a decade through editing and ghostwriting. After seeing author after author I've helped hold their book in their hands, I wanted to do that too! And this time, I wanted my name on those covers because there's nothing quite like that feeling. It's a bit surreal, but also gives you a surge of pride that all of your hard work and imaginings became something you could actually touch.

However, when I first started out, I had a lot of trouble finding what I wanted—information on writing clean *short* romance. You know, those stories that fall into the one-or two-hour reads category. Those delicious, bite-sized, not too big to finish in a day books that so many of our readers crave.

Short reads are incredibly popular among both authors and readers. Think of them as popcorn or chips or chocolate chip cookies. It's hard to stop at just one, and you always want more!

On the reader side, is there anything more satisfying than a complete story that gives you all the feels? One that makes your emotions soar, your stomach sink, and your heart start pounding? One that you are able to finish on a lunch break or while waiting in the car pickup line for your children? Thick books have their place, but so do bite-sized stories.

As an author, it means you can create a single story or a series of them without a huge time commitment. You can create entire worlds and endless connected (or not) characters and feed them to your readers rapidly, quickly building your following, expanding your backlist, and fueling your creativity. You have that motivating feeling of getting your book out there to the world sooner than if you were writing longer length fiction.

There are many fantastic books about writing, and the same goes for marketing. There are also a few great books on writing shorter fiction. But...in talking to my friends and fellow authors, they all mentioned the thing that was lacking in those for them. The books weren't specifically about writing *clean* romance.

Why is that an issue? Because there are many who don't know where to start with writing, and worry that the information in those books may not be applicable to what they want to write. Sweet, swoony romance where the bedroom door is shut. Not chapters about how to write on-page intimacy and the buildup or complicated feelings afterward, since not all authors are comfortable about writing or reading that. Then, there's the other problem. If they were to skip writing those chapters, could they still deliver a story their readers would crave?

One woman asked me, "How is it even possible to keep tension on the page without sex?" Another said, "I have no idea where to even start with writing short romance. I just know I want to, and I want to keep it clean."

As you keep reading, I'm going to cover both of those worries, and so much more. We're going to start all the way at the beginning, before you've even picked up a pen or started typing, and I'll walk you through all the way to the end, when you've got your finished story and need to figure out what to do with it.

It's my hope that everyone who picks this book up—experienced author or new—walks away with some valuable information so that the books you are dreaming about become reality.

Now, there's something very important you must know about this book. I'm not going to tell you how to write. Nope. That's your department! What I'm going to do is tell you the different elements that you need to consider having to create your story from idea to finished product to getting it out into the world. The actual writing part is up to you. Think of these pages as a recipe. You'll find the ingredients here in this book, but it's up to you to combine them.

I'm also not going to tell you how to run your business. There's no info about schedules and choosing to be in Kindle Unlimited versus wide, and how to set yourself up for success with data analysis or maximizing preorders. The only business talk you'll find is what to do after your book is done, like what to think about when it comes to choosing keywords and covers, editors, and cheap or free marketing tips.

These pages have all the things you need to get started. Even better, it's in one place, just like I wish I'd had when I first started writing.

As with any skill or business, as you grow, you'll expand. But growth and expansion can be overwhelming. It's my goal to keep this simple, so that you aren't overwhelmed, and can feel confident in writing bite-sized romance, no matter the subgenre.

Grab sticky notes or a highlighter and feel free to mark up your book because it's going to help you get from idea to book baby in your hands.

Are you ready? Let's get going!

PART 1: THE CORE CONCEPTS OF CLEAN SHORT ROMANCE

DEFINING CLEAN ROMANCE

We're going to start this chapter by getting some questions out of the way. First up? What is clean romance?

When you start digging into that question, you'll see that the definition of *clean* can vary, depending on the author. That's why there are generally heat levels, even within clean romance. The Writing Gals created a fantastic guide to those. Google will point you to it, but essentially clean romance is a story where there is no sex on the pages. The romance between your couple is going to be focused more on the emotional and relational development between them than on the sexual one.

Now, this doesn't mean that there is no act of attraction. There's got to be romance in a romance book, right? This is why you'll sometimes see phrases tacked onto a book description such as "kisses only" or "closed door" or "no spice." Some authors want to keep the tension going for their couple and the readers with just hand holding, a well-timed (or interrupted!) kiss, or a teasing look. Others might show a higher level of desire, with a deep kiss but nothing explicit.

Your heat levels are for you to decide. Do you need to have spice in order to write a great book? Nope! Do you need to have tension, sexual or not? Yes! But...bringing those feels, those emotions to your reader, comes from writing skill, not spicy words.

Readers love clean reads (so don't let anyone trick you into thinking they aren't popular!) for many different reasons. A few I've been told are:

- I like that my teen can read them too.

- I love how I get to focus on the emotional connection and the character depth.

- These books are usually so heartwarming.

- It's nice not to worry about something triggering in the pages.

- I don't feel embarrassed if someone sees what I'm reading.

- The slow burn and anticipation are my favorite!

- It's relatable. We don't all fall in bed the second we see someone.

- The books align with my personal/religious views.

- I love a good story.

The list goes on, but even if it didn't, there are so many reasons why readers love clean romance.

Now, let's talk about short romance, and why it's so appealing. Is shorter bad? Oh heck no! Short and sweet (just like you are going to be writing) has so, so many benefits, and it's both enjoyable for the reader and the author. Once you start poking around in author groups, you'll even see just how many women support or contribute to their family's finances by writing shorter books.

If the phrase "short romance" is new to you, chances are you've heard it called something else in the romance genre, like short story, novelette, or novella. The "rules" of writing romance are the same, no matter the length. The things you need in it—including the Happily Ever After (HEA) or Happy for Now (HFN)—are also the same. Just, the story is told at a single point in time, instead of spanning something much longer, and, of course, the word count is much, much smaller.

How much smaller?

A short story is a complete story, told between 1,000 and 7,500 words. A novelette is just above that, with 7,500 words up to 17,500 words. Lastly, we have the novella (which is the category I write in) and those books start at 17,500 words and go up to 40,000.

All of these are sweet-spot categories on Amazon. They easily fit in the short reads categories Amazon created, which allows readers to hunt for a book based on the amount of time they have to read: 15 minutes, 30 minutes, 45 minutes, 1 hour, 90 minutes, or 2 hours or more. These are the exact category names, so it's easy to Google or pop over to Amazon and search Short Reads to pull up that list.

How are the short reads categories determined? It's done by page count. Formatting can change that slightly.

Generally, to be in the 15-minute reads category, your book must be 1 to 15 pages. In the 30-minute category, the length is 12 to 21 pages, and so on. Now, I'm going to be quite upfront and honest. The ways of KDP are mysterious, vague, and often change. So, there's no telling what system they use to calculate a page's length, because if you've ever published something on Amazon, in eBook and paperback, you'll see they are never, ever the same page length, but that's the info from their website. This also isn't a category you get to choose. Amazon puts you there. I'll revisit this in Chapter 18.

Once your book is over 40,000 words in length, it's no longer considered a novella. Your book would be long enough to fully develop any story's plot, and you wouldn't have the need to quickly get your couple together or even start right in the moment of their meet-cute. You'd be able to have not just a mention of a backstory, but also show it on page, and you'd allow for more and deeper character, world, or relationship development.

What does that mean if you want to write these shorter lengths? It means that readers of short romance have *expectations*. They want the meet-cute quickly, they want the plot to keep moving, and they don't want to be bogged down by details. Readers want the whole story and all its necessary parts, like the conflict, the all is lost moment, and the happily ever after or happy for now. And...they want it in that shorter word count so they can go on to your next story and your next one—all in between the tedious life events that they need to do.

But does short fiction really sell? Yes. Yes, it does. At a shocking rate. Why?

Think about it...what makes waiting to be called back at an appointment better? Or in the school pickup line? Or while you are waiting for your grocery pickup?

Why, a bite-sized story to sink your teeth into, of course! It's far more enjoyable than doom-scrolling your feed and seeing things that stress you.

There's so much more to cover, though, so let's keep going. Now that you know what short romance is, let's talk about one of the tricky things…making it realistic.

Creating Believable Short Romance

Picture this. Carrie is walking down the aisle at the grocery store, and spots the last jar of her favorite salsa. As she reaches for it...someone else does too. There are sparks. A tingle that runs through her hand, makes butterflies in her stomach start to fly, and before you know it, they are at a little café, each with a warm drink and gazing into the other's eyes. This is it. He's *the one.*

Realistic? Not really. There's actually a lot wrong with the paragraph above. But, it's a good base, and we can make it realistic. How? Let me show you, my friend.

First, remember; your story might be short, but it still needs all of the critical story elements. You might be starting *in media res*, which is a Latin phrase that means in the middle of things, but that isn't a bad thing. It doesn't mean your story won't have all the good stuff that readers love. Quite the opposite, actually. It means that every word counts, and you are going to use them to their full potential to make your writing stand out and keep your readers on the edge of their seats. Your book is *only* going to have the good stuff!

Want to see how?

Let's take the same plot, and add the story elements you are going to learn about in this book. We can make it realistic by not only adding the backstory that's left off the pages, but also relatable emotions and conflicts. But it doesn't have to be pages and pages worth. Nope, we can keep this moving along at a good pace, give your readers what they want, but keep that page length smaller so you can get your word count to fall into that category you want to be in. And, just as importantly...we are going to make this swoon worthy. You ready?

Carrie's walking through the grocery store trying not to cry. Her last unmarried friend just called. It's official. Carrie is an unwanted and unloved single woman and the last of her friend group to have someone serious. Might as well buy some snacks to drown her sorrows. And a cat. Maybe three. Then she'd have a good excuse never to be seen in public again. All that litterbox duty, you know.

As she reaches for the jar of salsa, someone else does the same. Her eyes narrow, and she is about to have a tug of war over the last extra spicy pineapple habanero salsa, because she NEEDS it, when her eyes widen, her lips part in surprise, and she says, "Donny?"

That's right. It's Donny Sterling. Her best friend who moved away just before high school and she lost track of. The guy who knew all her secrets. And now, he's making her hand tingle. Could this be the sign she's been waiting for from the universe?

Wait. Nope. Never mind. That's her phone vibrating with another text from Susan. It's going to be a destination wedding in Hawaii. Bring a date.

Carrie can't help it, she starts to sniffle, and Donny, the one who always knew her better than she knew herself, whispers, "Hey, what's going on?"

But she shakes her head, not wanting to talk in front of strangers, and he leads her to the store's café, where over a steamy cinnamon latte she tells him, "I don't have a date. I don't even have a boyfriend. I have nothing. I'm such a loser."

Donny smiles and shakes his head. "No way. You have me. I'll be your plus one."

Alright...that's looking better, isn't it? It's feeling more believable because now we know Carrie has a few problems. And, while it's not entirely plausible the guy she hasn't seen for years is right there in town, it could be. "Could" is the keyword.

Donny could turn out to be a billionaire after a tech startup success. He could have been offered a job, could be just passing through and hoping to have run into some old friends… He could be a musician touring around. It doesn't really matter why he's there, if it's believable.

And…quick interruption. This goes for historical (my preferred genre) stories too. While this is a modern setting, Carrie could be in a general store. Donny could be stopping into town, after he was just driving cattle or breaking horses or returned from leading settlers on the Oregon Trail. The year and the setting don't matter. It's the conflicts and the tropes, and making them believable.

Carrie's problem (being single, feeling miserable about it, having no one to take to the wedding) feels real. A few details (specific salsa, cats for an excuse, her phone vibrating) but not so many it uses all your word count, add to the realism. It's also the perfect setup. At this point, as long as it's realistic-feeling, anything goes to get your couple together.

We already know this is going to be a friends to lovers story just from this initial setup. It's the *how are they going to get there* we don't know. Yet.

No matter what you write to bring them together, since we have a little bit of a backstory that happened off page and can be told in just a few sentences, we now have:

- A believable situation

- Believable characters

- The perfect romantic plot

But short romance is a little more than just laying eyes on a past friend or lover or even a stranger or celebrity and things working out perfectly for your couple. Nope! If that's all that happened, the story would be boring. And over in like...two pages.

Life isn't perfect, it's messy. It's full of stresses. You've got your internal factors that cause conflicts and the external ones. (We're going to go more in depth with this in a later chapter, but it's important to touch on it right now.)

Internal conflicts can be everything from the stories your character tells themselves about not being good enough to fears, insecurities, and emotional wounds like the inability to trust someone. External factors are ones they don't have control over. This is their job stress, the weather, a car breaking down.

Regardless of what it is, it's these stresses and these conflicts that also add to your story and make it *believable*. It creates an emotional connection between the reader and your character. It's also going to be what makes it good, and makes your reader come back for more.

You've got to have all the things a novel-length book would have, just in bite-size.

If Carrie and Donny go to the wedding, have a dance, and lock eyes and he proposes, that's not very satisfying, is it? It also isn't going to make your reader want to turn the pages of another of your stories.

The reader knows that Carrie and Donny are going to get together in the end. But...they want it earned. They want it real. They want to see some struggle first. It's human nature. We like to see others have that incredible thing happen for them after they've suffered unfairly.

Let's head back to the story and do a time jump. It's a month later, during which time they've not gotten together in person, but Donny has promised Carrie by text and calls that he will be there no matter what. Carrie is there at the wedding spot, and Donny's supposed to arrive any moment.

What could go wrong? What can push them together in a realistic and satisfying way to move them from friend zone to romantic partners?

Maybe while she's waiting, her friends start teasing her. They tell her she's lying...she doesn't have a date. In fact, she never has dates. She's feeling really crummy and down on herself. Carrie is also freaking out. She can show she's not a total loser if Donny just hurries up and gets there! He should have arrived an hour before. Now, she's feeling even worse. She's never, never going to have a boyfriend, not when she can't even get a friend to show up and pretend he's dating her. Her life is awful.

Pause. Let's dissect this. So, what's happening here? We've got some conflict building. She's all alone, even though Donny promised. He's not there, she's getting teased, and she's so down on herself. This makes your story believable. It's also making the reader want to keep turning the pages to find out what's going to happen, right? Will he show up? Will she get her HEA or HFN? Are her friends going to stare with dropped jaws because her date, Donny, is the head of the most famous rock group ever?

We don't want to leave them, or you, hanging, so let's keep going.

Just then, the wedding starts. Carrie is there, a fake smile plastered as her friend walks up the aisle. Meanwhile, she is wondering just how soon she can pretend she's got a headache and escape during the reception. She keeps waiting, but no Donny. The wedding is over, the cake cut. Still no Donny.

Everyone starts breaking into couples to dance. Just as she can't take it anymore, and starts to slip out a side door, she bumps into someone. It's Donny! His rental car had broken down, but he pulls her into his arms, twirling her around the room, apologizes like crazy, and tells her how he wouldn't miss this for anything. "Not because I'm doing you a favor," he whispers, pulling her closer, "but because it means I get to hold you in my arms. Carrie...there's something I've wanted to tell you for years. I love you. I always have."

Annnd there it is. The swoon! The happy ending! The much more believable story. A romance that has all the feels because it was earned by the couple having a realistic thing happen and realistic doubts and fears and worries.

Bite-sized romances can have any plot, any trope, as long as there is something that creates an immediate bond. This can be a fear, a past (off-page) moment or relationship, a rescue, a casual interaction with a stranger, or one of a dozen other "things" that causes an instant (but earned) attraction.

Best of all, this being clean romance, you get to focus on the building of those moments that bring them together, something that creates the heartwarming, swoony, sweet, addicting thing readers love...not just skip over those emotional needs your readers have (and your characters!) to get to the spicy stuff.

But...if you don't have that realism in your book, your story is going to struggle. Having believability is as critical as having words on the page.

Now, let's get to the next chapter and visit another important topic in writing short romance.

THE POWER OF TROPES

I'm going to be totally honest here, even if it's a little embarrassing. I still probably don't know all the tropes I put into my books. They aren't planned and they like to sneak up on me. I'm an intuitive writer, and I'm a total pantser. What I'm feeling is what goes down, and my fingers have a mind of their own. So, the first time someone said, "I love how you had this trope and that trope and that trope too," I was all, "Uh. Yes. Thank you. I thought that would work well."

Psst. I didn't. I had no idea. I was just writing down the things the characters in my mind were doing. Things I liked. Things I thought would work well, based on the story I was crafting. I wasn't TRYING to hit the tropes.

They were just popping out subconsciously. I still write that way, even though I know they exist and are easy to look up if I get stuck on a story and need an idea.

Keep my secret, please?

That all said, there are many readers who adore particular tropes and will read any and everything with that trope. If you are writing to market or if you are wanting to brand yourself, then you might be wanting to stick with a handful of tropes and use them each time, especially if you find you enjoy writing them and the readers enjoy devouring them.

"Won't that get boring?" I hear you asking. "Doesn't that mean every single story is going to be the same?" Nope! That's just your trope, not your story details. I have written in a fair number of multi-author series collabs. They all have a single premise or theme we have to work with and each book needs to include it. Think mail-order bride, runaway bride, unrequited love, forbidden love, marriage of convenience, enemies to lovers. But...do you know what else those premises are? They are tropes!

The power of a trope is that it not only appeals to readers, but it gives you ideas for your story! No matter the trope, there is a way to use it in a story. And if you are cranking out (Quality! Crank it out but make it polished!) your bite-sized stories, then you might need some story ideas. That's where a trope can help. Let's say you like to write forced proximity romances. How many ways can you force your characters together?

The answer is as many as you can think of.

At work, stranded somewhere, at an event, because someone's sick, during a storm, one is a first responder, a doctor in an emergency, locked together in a room, on the PTA together, volunteering, assigned seats, etc. The list can go on and on and on...and do you know what else? Some of those things I just listed? Are also tropes. Workplace romance, that's a trope. Stranded/rescue me, that's a trope. The hero? Oh yeah. A trope.

There are some tropes that are much better at forcing that instant connection. Others work for a slower approach. Neither is wrong. But how many tropes do you need? Some authors say the more the better. And, if you can stick three or four or even five in your short story, go for it! But don't, and I repeat, *don't* use a trope just because you think it's what people want if it doesn't fit the story.

For example, if you are writing a short fantasy, and you have your hero going on a journey (trope!) then you might end up with a little forced proximity, right? (Also a trope.) One character could be grumpy, the other a ray of sunshine (trope!) and maybe opposites attract or there's forbidden love or one of them has a secret identity! Trope, trope, and trope!

Do you see how in that particular type of story, you could have that many tropes? It might not always be the case if you only have so many words to work with or a set idea, and something just wouldn't make sense to do. And, while a trope can run throughout your entire story, especially if you are writing a 5,000-word story where they are trapped during a snowstorm and there's only one bed and they absolutely hate each other, a trope may not always last longer than a scene or a chapter.

Before you add too many tropes, make sure that they are what Chapter 2 was all about—being believable. That's where knowing tropes can also help. There are some that work very well in short romance, and others that would be difficult to pull off.

For example, forced proximity, second chance, and fake dating work well in a short romance, but ones that need extensive worldbuilding or backstory to set up the romance are going to be much harder to pull off. Seek the tropes that you can make work well together within your needed word count.

If you know right away you want to use a fake marriage, enemies to lovers, grumpy/sunshine, or any other trope, then that's going to help you write your story. If you feel stuck, you can look at those tropes and say, "Okay: He could act like this because he hates her, and she's so freaking cheerful, and he has no idea how he's going to manage to marry her, even if it's fake."

For you plotters, knowing your tropes will help you plan out ideas and keep you from getting lost. Pantsers, don't fret! I've got you. You are my people. While you might not be planning out your tropes, I bet early on you're going to write one in, even if it's accidental, and being familiar enough to recognize it will help you keep the story on track. After all, if you see you've got a friends to lovers story starting, you are going to be able to write those awkward conversations, shy looks, the worry about screwing everything up, worries your characters have, and are going to make it feel realistic.

That's all well and great, you might be thinking. But how am I going to find some tropes to study and use? The back of this book, my friend. I've got a list of sixty tropes, and a brief description of them for you, for the ones you aren't familiar with. Study them, use them, become a trope master!

There are way more tropes out there, but this list will get you started. But are you ready to move on? Let's talk about your characters.

PART 2: BUILDING YOUR CHARACTERS

CREATING YOUR MAIN CHARACTERS

Part of the fun of writing is not just creating worlds and events, but the people who live in and shape them. In fact, it might just be my favorite part. Though we need to keep the story believable, if you craft your characters well, then they will be just that. They will connect with your readers, make them want to cheer or cry or be angry and think about them long after the story is over.

And that, my friend, is a good thing. You want your readers to feel like these characters are real because then they will want to read another of your books, and another.

So, let's talk about how to make your characters feel realistic, jump off the page to give the readers just what they want, and bring these fictional individuals to life. One of the most powerful tools for creating instant tension? Give your character two things they desperately want that oppose each other.

What do a pizza delivery guy and a young billionaire boss and a cowboy have in common? Ah, no, sorry. That's not the start of a joke. Ask my kids. I'm the least funny person they know. (Likely because they don't get dry humor!) No, these three men are something else. They each have the makings of a fantastic character for your books. They have conflicting desires, those two things they don't think they can have.

But is it enough to just choose names or jobs for characters? How are you going to make them ready for that instant falling-in-love moment? The answer to that is by first focusing on their desires, fears, and emotional wounds, then fleshing them out a tad more. We all have things we want, things we are scared of, and things that haunt us, so if you aren't sure who your characters are and the things they are struggling with, look around at the people you know or even yourself. What do you see?

Using the male character examples from above, let's come up with a few things that could be going on for them, so I can show you how these men are ready for their story to unfold and how opposing desires work.

Dropping off his first delivery of the day, the pizza guy is grateful he was given a good tip. Yesterday was slow, and he doesn't want a repeat of it. This delivery guy has an intense desire (which you'll find some people use interchangeably with the word goal) and is working hard to make it happen. He wants to get himself through college, get a good steady job, and help out his mom and little sister, after a sudden illness left his sister wheelchair-bound and his dad walked out, not wanting the responsibility anymore.

That's our first guy. Let's meet the second. In a huge sixty-story glass-windowed office building, our billionaire is looking out the window, wondering how he can do the impossible—please his father who owns the company and expects him to take over. The man isn't ever satisfied with anyone or anything, and is so critical, our hero is scared to admit the one thing he wants, and worries he's never going to have. And that's a wife and kids and the company...but run differently. Less cutthroat. More supportive of working parents.

It's time to meet the final man. Just outside a little diner, a cowboy is leaving, shoulders slumped after he was asked, again, if he was fully recovered. He used to love the feel of the wind on his face as he rode his horse, but after a terrible riding accident, he's going through life without purpose. He won't admit it to anyone, but even though he's cleared to get back on his strawberry roan, he's scared. He's taken falls before, but this one was serious. Life-changing. And if he can't overcome this fear, it's going to make him lose his ranch and all he cares about.

So, what do we have here with these three men? Each is quite different in their daily life, but each is similar in that he has a desire, a goal, a wanting to do something or have something. Each also has a conflict. Something that is standing in the way or making things more difficult in their life. They each have an emotional wound. Something personal in nature that happened to them or weighs on them, and they have to overcome it in order to determine their future.

There's something else too. Love. One has mentioned wanting a relationship, but the others haven't. So, you've got a few ways you can do a setup for the romance aspect. A character can actively be looking for love, it can take them by surprise, or they can try and avoid it...but fail. And, if you look closely, you've got several tropes going on to help guide your characters and their story, all hidden there in their desires and conflicts.

When I first brought these three characters to you, what were you thinking? Just basic guys, right? But when we created a little bit of a backstory, bringing forth those elements to make them believable, they came to life. In fact, these guys are just about bursting off the page and are ready for you to tell their story and find them the perfect girl to give them an HEA or HFN.

We don't need to take a long time to introduce the right woman. Word count, right? She might already be there or walking around the corner. Here's what I mean:

The cute pizza maker, who admires how hard our delivery guy works. The office intern, who hates seeing her boss so miserable, and knows that's why he's always so grumpy. The single mom whose daughter is just crazy about horses, and volunteers at the cowboy's ranch, just to spend time with them.

Creating characters that will be believable and also have a connection with your readers doesn't have to be hard, but it's an important part of writing, and the very heart of compelling fiction, no matter the word count.

If that still feels overwhelming to do, here's a suggestion. We aren't all the same, right? If you walk into your local fast food place, what will you see? People of all ages, shapes, and sizes, and all dressed differently. Listen as they place their orders. Some might say thanks, others thank you; some might just walk away silently after getting their change. For sure, you're even going to have some rude or angry ones at the counter.

But you know this, right? So why am I asking you? It's because just like in the real world, your on-page people aren't all going to be the same. You'll need to be able to express that. Your character's desires, conflicts, and wounds are a needed thing in your story—and a fantastic start when you are preparing to write—but won't completely make your character.

In case you are a list person, like I am, let's write it out a little more so you've got the tools you're going to need to create your own swoon-worthy but totally realistic characters.

The Character Deep Dive

In order to make our characters believable, we are going to need to be sure they have certain things. Think of this as a recipe. We've got to have our ingredients, so it's time to get baking. Let's go over what your character needs.

Conflicting Desires

Our billionaire is the perfect example for this. He wants a wife and kids one day, but he also wants control of the company he's been promised since childhood. Can a man running a massive company have that when every minute of his day needs to be spent at the office and managing people?

By having these conflicting desires, two things he wants, it makes it all the more real. The struggle is right there, preventing him from having both things he wants. And if he chooses just one, he knows his life won't be complete.

He will have regrets. So, that increases his stress and makes him tell himself the lie that he can't have both. There's no way. He's got to choose.

Flaws or Traits

A good flaw or trait in a character isn't just that the pizza delivery guy is obsessed with keeping his delivery vehicle clean or tucks his shirt in. You aren't looking for a cute little quirky or annoying habit. You are wanting the thing that is preventing them from achieving their goal. For example, our pizza guy puts in overtime every chance he gets and always covers for others.

That's not a nice-guy habit, that's him so focused on what he's wanting (money to help his family and pay for college) that it's preventing him from spending time with those who love him or who want to love him. Like the cute pizza maker or anyone else who has their eye on him. The flaw, being too consumed with his job and making money, will affect his story and be something he needs to overcome for his HEA.

How? That's up to you, but some of my thoughts on that are maybe he works until past the point of exhaustion and ends up making mistakes, sabotaging himself. Maybe he skips meals, to try and save money, wanting every dollar to go to his family. Regardless of what it is, his two desires are having trouble coexisting.

The Core Belief or Lie They Tell Themselves

We all have stories we tell ourselves or others. What's theirs? Our cowboy might be thinking that if he can't get back in the saddle, he can't run his ranch. People will think he's weak. Useless. And even if he ever did want to have a girlfriend, who is going to want a man like him?

Now, you and I know the things he's thinking and worrying about are not true. But, it sounds realistic, doesn't it? Chances are even good you or someone you know has said something similar in their life. If they/you can't ABC, then people will think XYZ. We are all pretty aware of cause and effect. It might help to think of the core belief or lie they tell themselves as that. This is something else that has to be overcome, both for the satisfying story and the romance to happen.

This core belief is such an important part of the conflicting desires. While often in life we do have to choose one thing over another, when it's a small thing, like a soda flavor, or a color choice, it's not a big deal. But when it's a choice between moving for our dream job or staying to care for an aging loved one? Much harder. Life-changing. This is what you are going for.

Specific Dialogue

Remember people-watching in the fast food place? Everyone was different, and your characters are too. Give each of them a unique voice that's shaped by their background. Our billionaire is going to speak very differently than our cowboy will. After all, an Ivy upbringing is quite different from the School of Hard Knocks.

Is your character from a state where there's a lot of twang in their voice? Do they speak in slang? Gesture a whole lot? Interrupt themselves or stammer? Speak in short sentences? You don't need to write the stutter or the twang into every sentence. Just a time or two gets the point across. The point is just to make your characters distinct, and not as though each man or woman came from the same cookie cutter in your mind.

If it's hard for you to imagine, and you do better with seeing something firsthand, start by thinking about the people you know or get a little people-watching in, and use how they act for some inspiration.

Show Their Tell

What's something your character does to show stress or that they are lying? Is there a necklace they fidget with? A pen they click? Maybe they don't meet someone's eyes or pinch the bridge of their nose, steeple their fingers.

Small physical actions make your characters feel like a real person, and create a visual image for your reader. These little mannerisms will also do more than just add personality or vivid imagery. They can *show* your reader how the characters are feeling without you *telling* the reader. That keeps your story moving forward in an active voice since you only have so many words to work with, instead of slowing it down and putting your book in a longer category.

We all know how to write that someone's happy. But writing with a giggle, a grin that hurts their face, and clapping hands together with a little bounce is a lot more visual and connects your reader to the character. It brings them to life.

Secrets, Secrets, Secrets

We all have secrets, right? Something we don't want others to know. What would happen if it got out? What do they do to make sure someone doesn't know about that secret? How far are they willing to go or act to keep it to themselves?

Whatever it might be, having a secret and trying to keep it as such adds stress and tension, and is a part of what will dictate your character's decisions throughout the story, for good or bad. It's also one more way to make your character believable. After all, don't you act a little differently when you are trying to keep something to yourself?

Secrets can be anything from trying to hide something they don't like to a traumatic event to a secret baby to being allergic to a cat because they really want to be with the guy at the pet shelter. Secrets don't always have to be huge and life-changing. They can also be sweet and endearing because your character is putting their own discomfort aside, to be with the one they are attracted to.

Stress Reactions

How does your character react to stress? Do they become aggressive? Run away and try to avoid conflict? Freeze and start to stammer? Heart racing? Sweaty palms? Hands curling into fists? Speechless? Cry?

Remember, too, that not all stress reactions are bad ones. That's a really important thing to note. Losing your job? Bad. Surprise party? Could go either way. The crush telling you he loves you? Good. But your body is still experiencing that stressful moment, so be sure to show it in the writing by making your character act appropriately.

Just like the show your tell, you don't want to just say someone is stressed. You want to show what stressed looks like for them personally. It's not the same for everyone. And, if they are showing a physical sign, like clammy hands, are they doing something about it to try and hide it? Like wiping them on their jeans? Hoping their palm is not damp as they reach for a handshake?

Give Non-Plot Interests

To help with the realism of your fictional person, give them something more than their job or their problem. What things do they do when they aren't working or stressing out about stuff? Can you have dozens of pictures they've taken and framed on the wall? A karate trophy on a shelf? A huge library with well-worn covers on the classics? A collection of hats or watches? Do they have every Saturday morning booked on the calendar so that they can volunteer at the homeless shelter?

Even if it's not brought up but in a very small way, having these details rounds out your character, and makes them more lifelike. Don't forget about the mundane details. Their lunch order. How every Tuesday they eat tacos. That in the afternoon, it's always a soda for a pick-me-up, or each morning starts with a hot drink.

Did you get some good ideas from that list? Depending on the length of your book, you might not have room for all of that. I completely understand that a short story only 3,000 words long doesn't have the word count available like a 13,000-word novelette does. However, if you have the room, remember that all of these things will make your characters realistic, which then helps make your plot believable. I can't stress that point enough, which is why I keep saying it.

There's one more thing to mention, and that's the character point of view, or POV. Some authors like to write from only one point of view. If that's what you choose, you might need more dialogue to expose how the other character is feeling. Other authors like dual POV for their main characters. This lets you get a deeper look at how your character is thinking or feeling.

I want you to have success with your writing, and the best way to get readers coming back for more is to create characters that feel real and make your reader think about them after the story is over.

But your main female and main male aren't the only ones in the story. Let's talk next about supporting character roles.

SUPPORTING CHARACTER ROLES

While your main characters are, well, the main (meaning most important!) characters, the supporting characters are also important. You might have also heard them referred to as side characters. Many times, they are the ones who help push the couple together or else give dozens of reasons why it's a bad idea...maybe even the ones causing the conflict that your story needs. Depending on the length of your story, they can also tie standalone books into a series.

Let's talk about each of those roles, and how they can be used to elevate a simple story into something richer for your reader.

Keep in mind, above all else, your story must be believable. So, if you are writing a story that's 5,000 words in length, you might not have the ability to have a whole supporting cast. You might need to keep everything tightly focused on the couple. That's okay. You never, never want to do anything that will take away from the main story.

But how can a supporting character help your story? In three ways! They can push the main characters together, attempt to split them apart, or be used as a recurring character to build a series.

Your side characters can come in many forms. They might be a family member, like a parent, sibling, cousin, etc. It's possible they are a best friend...or a rival.

Nothing feels more realistic than a friend playing matchmaker or a jealous rival stirring up trouble. A side character has so much power in your story, it's important to use it to help push your characters together. However, one thing you don't want to do is make them all the same. Do you remember earlier, when I brought up the hypothetical situation of people walking into a fast food restaurant, and how everyone acted differently? Just because your side character isn't a main one, doesn't mean that they should be any less realistic. They, too, will have personalities and traits about them. They shouldn't fade into the background to be a carbon copy of your other characters.

While there might not be the word count to put much of that on the page in a very short romance, if you are writing something 20,000 words long, then you'll need those characters to be a little bit more fleshed out, even if the line here or there only equals a single page in the entirety of your book. Sometimes, it's those small things that make your character, supporting or not, feel real.

This might be oversimplifying, but I think that generally you can put your supporting characters into two broad categories. Those with positive traits and those with negative traits. Some of you might want to break those down into even smaller groups, perhaps classified by similarities, and feel free to do so, but those two classifications are still going to be the same, no matter how you break things down further. It's like the classic good versus evil.

Positive (good) trait side characters are going to do things like introduce your main character to someone, be the encourager, and tell them to stop making excuses. They'll watch the single mom's baby, support her when her boss is giving her a hard time, take him over some dinner when he's been sick, stand up for them when someone says something rude…The list could go on and on. This character is the one who is always going to be on their friend's (or family member's) side. No matter what.

The positive supporting character also might agree to go to the movies with her and two guy friends, but then get a stomach bug, and hey! What do you know? One of the guys had to work late, so it's just your main character and her crush. Between being a help with an idea or a rescuer just in time or just being encouraging, they also might be a little sneaky in ways to set the main characters up. All things that your main character needs.

But what about the negative trait supporting character? That's going to be the villain, the rival, the overly protective family member or friend, the jealous ex. The one who has dozens of reasons why your main character should not get into a romance. There's a lot of fun to be had with that. Is the rival saying not to get in the romance with someone because they really like the main character? Do they know something important that would be a deal breaker for the main character and they want to protect them?

Or, is it a jealousy thing, and they know the two main characters are meant to be together and want to do everything in their power to keep them apart? And, why? There's so much they can do that brings the conflict to separate or bring together the main characters.

Obviously, characters like these will have bigger roles in your book. But what about when you just need someone to be there in the background? The person running the café, the bus (or stagecoach!) driver, the store cashier. There are a few things you can do, like just have them there, nameless and hanging out in the background, or you can make them a part of your books that take place in the same town. No matter what you choose, their existence, and existing always in the same place or in the same capacity, makes your town feel more real. In some instances, it can even bring some humor to the situation.

Have you ever watched *Peppa Pig*? Miss Rabbit works what, a zillion jobs? And how funny it was to see her over in one place, say goodbye, and then see her in another place just a moment later! Though my kids have not watched that show for years, she stands out to me simply because of how amusing that was, and how I always looked for her to appear in multiple places throughout the episode because you never knew what she'd do next.

Your town's characters may even lead into something more one day; you never know. To my surprise, an aging ranch hand named Gus, whom I put in one of my books as a supporting character popping up here and there telling folks the forecast with his weather knee, became so popular that I was getting asked if he could have his own story or at least give him bigger roles in my books!

Because of his popularity, Gus will be getting his own book. Another set of standalones also developed into their own little town, where Maggie who runs the café, and Gabriel, the reverend, and Peter, the postmaster, each started to share more and more of their stories and...you guessed it, either have or will be getting their own book, and the whole town—that was started just to fill a need—will get a series.

It's important to note I didn't fill my first standalone books with names and the intention of creating a series. And, when I revisited that town, I didn't know if a series was in its future, but little by little, a new face popped in, and along with it the thing they were known for, and it just naturally grew. There was no info dump. No cast of so many characters we couldn't keep straight who was who. It was all written in bite-sized books, around 25,000–30,000 words in length for each.

And, if you do want to have characters who reappear over and over, it's okay to remember they don't need to be in every book. My characters don't always need to visit the post office. If they do, Peter is there. They don't always need to visit the café, but if they do, Maggie or Carissa are there. I've taken standalone titles and made a little town. My readers like knowing when we go to the café, they'll be greeted with Maggie's cider or Carissa's pies. It's a cozy, familiar thing for them, and serves to make the characters and their town realistic.

If you have standalone titles, and you think you'd like to try and make them a series to encourage read-through, that's where these side characters can help. Pick a standalone, and look for someone's name. If you hadn't named them, but they are a waitress or something else, in the book you are writing right now, give her a name and have one of your characters say: "Hey, so and so!" That makes her part of your world and no longer nameless. You can do this for the town doctor, the postman, café owner, etc. And, it lets you connect your books for more read-through or for box set collections.

These characters might be small, but they are still important. By having them appear now and again for a moment in a story, readers of your previous books get excited to see them. They also add...here's that word again...realism. After all, don't you often see the same checker at the store? The same order taker? The same mail carrier? The same neighbors?

If you are having trouble thinking how to work that side character into your book, but you know you need them either to expand your word count or to bring together or separate your couple, think of those you know personally and have interacted with. Or, go with the classic traits and work from there. A gossip, a pessimist. That annoyingly sunshiny person. The jock, the man who always jogs at six a.m. in a yellow tank top, the dog walker with more dogs than she can handle, the older woman feeding the ducks.

The list can go on and on, endlessly. One of the best parts of being an author is that you are never without material or inspiration, and an hour or two of people-watching can give you pages full of ideas for characters. Whatever you do, though, don't make them faceless. Give them something, a name, a look (the woman with the glasses that always fall, the girl with the pink hair, the old man who walks around with a newspaper) so that in the future, if you decide to, you can build on those characters and make them a deliberate part of your writing world.

THE IMPORTANCE OF INTERNAL DIALOGUE AND MONOLOGUE

Have you ever wished you were a fly on the wall? There's a conversation you'd just love to be in on... Or, maybe you overheard something and can't stop thinking about it and the way it affected you. That feeling, that deep look into the thoughts and emotions, including positive or negative ones, is what we want to create with internal dialogue or monologue.

Though the names are similar, there's a pretty big difference between the two. Internal dialogue is that conversation we are having with ourselves. When we are in a conversation with someone, and our brain thinks/says: *Yeah, right.* Or our main female character sees the guy she likes walking down the street and thinks: *I just wish that were me.* Internal dialogue is short; it's thoughts; it's a line or two.

Internal monologue is longer. It's as though a narrator is the one talking. Let's use the example I just shared. The main female character sees the guy she likes walking down the street and thinks: *I just wish that were me.* Her internal monologue might be something like this.

I watched as he went down the street, laughing at something the other woman said. If only that were me instead. It didn't matter his jokes were horrible and he always messed up the punchline. I'd laugh. I'd do anything just to walk with him and hold his hand. But things never worked out the way I'd wanted. Not once.

Now, a very important note on your internal dialogue or internal monologue. Depending on what point of view you write in, that is going to change how your internal thoughts are also written and whether they are italicized or not. Here's how that works.

- **First person:** Internal thoughts blend naturally with narrative, so no italics are needed.

- **Third person:** Italics for direct thoughts can be used or just blended into the narrative.

- **Deep POV:** Thoughts flow seamlessly without italics or "he/she thought" tags.

That's all a style choice, and I'm not here to tell you how to write, only to share the elements of what you need to include in your bite-sized romance, and how to bring it into the world. This is a question I get asked a lot, though, so it felt like a good spot to add it in. However, I'm a firm believer in author style choices, and I'll say that all day long.

But if I did...we'd never finish this book and get you all the other info you needed! Let's get back to the importance of internal dialogue or internal monologue. I'm going to share some of the ways I love to use internal dialogue or internal monologue, but first, a warning.

In short romance, internal thoughts are powerful—so use them strategically. Too much introspection can stall your story when you only have 10,000 words to work with. But what are some of the best ways to use these little tools in your author toolbox?

Revealing Subtext and Inner Conflict

Internal thoughts allow your reader to see the gap that's created between what the character is saying, and what they are really thinking or feeling. For example, when she's saying thank you to someone who's "complimenting" her dress, and we all know she's not being complimented. Or, when she's saying hello to her blind date, but her thoughts are on hoping she remembered deodorant because she's sweating and that she's not going to throw up because she's so nervous.

By having that contrast between what a character is doing and what they are thinking, we give a bit more to the reader about who that character is. And we make them believable or relatable.

Controlling the Pace and Tension

This is one of my favorite techniques to do in a book, especially when it comes to internal thoughts. When used strategically, your character's internal dialogue or monologue controls the pace of the scene and the tension level. When your character stops to think about something, agonizing over a question just asked or a decision they are being forced to make, phew! That ups the tension in a scene. The reader is now right there with him or her as they think: well, is this the best choice? And they go over all the reasons why it's not a good idea.

On the other hand, if we've had some setup showing how eager and excited they are, we can speed up that moment, with one person starting to ask a question, and the other interrupting to give an answer.

This is one of those tools you don't want to overuse. Done too much, it loses the power it possesses. However, used at a critical moment, it's gold.

Showing Character Arcs

The internal narrative of your character is the only place readers can witness a character's genuine change or transformation. Outward actions change because their internal belief system has shifted, and the monologue is the window into that internal shift. If that felt a little confusing, let me explain it better.

When a reader is inside a character's head, they are that character. They feel each thing the character does, from sadness to elation. This is important for that reader-character connection. I know I've said that before, but it's so important, I want to make sure you hear it again.

In the next chapter, I'm going to go over how to show, not tell, in your book, but let me touch on that slightly here. Internal dialogue is perfect for showing things. We learn information about that character from their recalling a memory, or reading a letter, or noticing this item or that. For example, ballet slippers from a recent performance or paint supplies scattered on a table.

That keeps your readers from getting a huge info dump. The revelation about your character and who they are and the things they feel comes naturally, and goes into the story with ease. It makes your character more realistic, draws the reader into their life, from start to finish, and makes them part of the story, not an outsider looking in.

There's one more very important thing about internal dialogues or monologues. They create tension, conflict, and elevate emotional stakes for your character and the reader. Those are all things you're going to have a deep dive on in the next part of this book. But before we go deeper into conflict and emotional stakes, let's address a technique that will make all of this work: showing versus telling.

HOW TO SHOW, NOT TELL

Has it ever confused you when someone's said you are telling in your story, not showing? Isn't writing, well, writing? What's the difference? And why does it matter? Isn't the whole point of showing what's going on telling about it?

Not quite. Here's the difference.

Telling is like narrating. It's stating the facts. Showing is describing and drawing the reader in. Each has a purpose, but unless your book is primarily narrative in its style (which short form romance really doesn't have room to be) then you need to be showing, not telling what's happening.

Even if you have the room, which do you think would be more engaging for the reader? When you are reading a book, you don't want to be told what's happening. You want to experience it. The best and most memorable books that you've likely read have been those where you practically were there, on page with the main character.

So, it's important that you give that experience to your reader as well. That's what is going to make them want to continue to read your stories, over and over, and not just read them, but tell others how great they are.

Ready to learn some great tips for making your short romance stand out from the rest by showing and not telling?

Focus on the Five Senses

Instead of stating a condition (telling), describe the sensory input a character is experiencing (showing). Don't say she was angry. Show it. Her hands curl into fists. She slams the door. Her jaw clenches.

Don't say when he walked in the kitchen it smelled good. Mention the warm, yeasty bread smell. How his stomach rumbled in hunger. How cinnamon and other spices hung in the air.

It's not just a hot, sunny day. The sun is almost blinding, and she regretted not bringing her sunglasses as her eyes watered. Perspiration was already forming on her skin, and she hoped no one would notice the damp strands of hair clinging to her neck.

This can be done for each of the senses, and really brings the moment to life! Using details, instead of generic descriptions, can help set the scene or tone for your book. Instead of a messy car, you can mention discarded fast food wrappers, nearly empty bottles that are deformed from being stepped on. Dust so thick on the back bumper, it's tempting to draw in it.

Use Body Language and Actions

I'm guilty of it, so I bet you are too. Our characters smile. They laugh. They are so darn repetitive at times in their actions. So, let's replace some of those telling words (happy, sad, nervous, tired) with the specific physical reactions that demonstrate that emotion.

Instead of telling how anxious he was, let's show him pacing. Tapping his fingers. Instead of how tired she is, let's show her rubbing her eyes, yawning, her eyelids drooping.

What kind of body language might someone have when they are stressed? Impatient? Aggravated? And, how can you write that?

It's amazing how just that small addition to your story will elevate the moment, help the reader connect with the character's reactions more, and really bring a scene or emotion to life, while also giving a bit of an inside look at your character's mannerisms.

This is also a great thing to use for subtext. If your character says, "I'm fine," but she has her lips pressed together and crosses her arms, is she really? Her body language sure seems to be contradicting that. You could add a little internal dialogue or internal monologue here as well.

Choose Strong Verbs

Okay...I do this too sometimes. When we use a weak verb like walked, looked, laughed, etc., we are telling what's going on. There's nothing wrong with doing that sometimes. But if we do it all the time? We aren't really showing what's happening. We are narrating it, and like I said, that's telling, not showing.

This is where using physical descriptions really helps. A thesaurus is fantastic for this. So, instead of walking, they are ambling, or striding, or stomping, or slinking. Instead of looking, she's gazing, glaring, jerking her eyes in a direction. When it comes to laughing, we can chuckle, smirk, giggle, snort...the list goes on and on.

We are still doing the action, walk, look, laugh, but in a different way. A way that gives your reader a better visual, and keeps their mind engaged more in the story. An important note, though. Be careful not to overuse fancy verbs. Just having *walked* is sometimes perfectly fine. The goal in writing isn't to never use simple verbs—it's using stronger ones when the moment calls for it. You don't want every character sauntering and stalking everywhere, taking note of the cornflower blue sky, the cotton ball clouds, and the blazing golden sun or it becomes purple prose, which is flowery, over-the-top, and not as engaging to read. In other words, it's just too many descriptions both for verbs and adjectives.

Use Dialogue

This is a fantastic and simple way to not only give a deeper look into your characters, but also to show how they are feeling about something, instead of telling about it.

Say someone is meeting another person for lunch. You don't need to write: *She was tired of waiting for him and officially in a bad mood. He was an hour late.* You could show through dialogue, that same thing but in a more engaging, showing way. *"Took you long enough," she said. "I've been waiting an hour."*

By doing that, it also lets you show what the relationship is like between two people. You get the vibe she's upset right there. But what if she'd said: *"Finally! I'm starved."* Well, then the vibe would be different, and it's all told through the dialogue.

Breaking the Rule... Know When to Tell

Hold it... Didn't I just say how important it was to show? Now, I'm telling you that you can break the rule? Sure am! Let's be real. In 5,000-word stories, you'll tell MORE than in 40,000-word novellas. That's just a fact. You've got to make sure of your words and if that means a paragraph here or there of some backstory told through internal monologue, that's what it is.

Not every detail needs to be a cinematic scene where you are showing what's going on. Remember...limited word count, yeah? We're not going to show their time in high school together before he moved away and the ten years until they reconnected. This is when we are going to tell.

After high school, they imagined they'd go to the same college, spend the rest of their lives together. But when he moved in their senior year, and they lost contact with each other...

See? We just gave the backstory as a tell. It saves time and space. You can use your telling for moments or events in your story that are unimportant or simply to move the plot forward quickly. Another example of some phrases to speed things along, while also skipping unnecessary backstory could be: The next three years were a blur. Two months had passed. A few uneventful days later.

What we are doing is giving the story the time that it needs to progress logically, but making every word count. The trick is to show what is important in the story or has the potential to be an emotional moment. Tell what's necessary, but uneventful.

Here's another example. Instead of taking a chapter to show what a character is going through just after a breakup, we're going to tell it in a few lines, like this.

As she trudged down the street, Sally kept replaying that moment over and over again. When she'd accused him of cheating, he'd tried to explain it had been his sister, not a girlfriend. She hadn't listened, and now, after sleepless days and endless scrolling on socials—where she learned he was right and she was too quick to jump to conclusions—she couldn't stop thinking about the memories they'd made together over the last year, and how quickly she'd lost her chance to make more.

While we could have gone over those memories, and you could still hit a few, and we could have done a longer scene of her driving somewhere or talking about the stores she passed, each with a memory, there might not be space, and telling might need to be the rule.

Now that you've learned about building your world and your characters, it's time to put them together in the story arc.

PART 3: THE STORY ARC

SETTING THE SCENE

Did you know that the settings in your story are just as important as the characters themselves? It's true! Think of your favorite movies or TV shows during a romantic moment. Would it feel the same if there was nothing nearby? If they were in a sterile white-walled room, and the entire thing took place there? Yikes! That wouldn't be very enjoyable. Sure, they could do it. They are actors and actresses...but it's not quite the same in that plain room as in a crowded airport or under the stars or inside a taxi or swinging on a playground.

Since space is limited in your short fiction, be it a 3,000-word story or 25,000, every detail counts. Your setting shouldn't ever be just a backdrop. Make it an active participant in your story.

Feeling confused by that? Don't worry, it's much easier than it sounds. Let me break it down a little for you. Making a setting an active participant means that you are going to want to do the following:

Quickly Establish Core Elements

Remember, you may have few words to spare, so your reader needs to be plonked down in that setting right away. It's as though they have just walked in on what's happening or are seeing just what the character sees.

- **Place:** The specific physical location, with vivid details. For example, not an apartment, but a studio apartment overlooking the large maple tree in front of the bus stop. Not the beach, but the pebbled seaside with a chunk of driftwood that was turned into a bench everyone likes to sit on.

- **Time:** To prevent confusion, having the specific time period (1800s, 1920s, 500 years in the future, last month, yesterday, etc.) and also the time of the year (spring, winter, etc.) can help create the image in your reader's mind right away. With just the words: *A chilly wind swirled red and amber leaves down the sidewalk,* we aren't using too many words but really setting the scene. We know it's cold and we know it's fall. We don't know the year, but that's going to be obvious by either a contemporary short romance or else a historical one, where the year is usually put near the top of chapter one.

- **Social/Cultural Environment:** These are some additional details that serve to add not just to your scene, but also to your conflict! These setting details are things that affect the characters (cultural gender expectations, religious requirements, the living situation, such as a large family in a small home, or aunts and uncles living next door). Anything that adds to the understanding of your character, either in a positive or negative way.

As an example, in an early 1800s historical story, the fact that women couldn't own property creates immediate conflict. In a contemporary small-town romance, everyone knowing everyone's business adds pressure. These aren't just background details—they also help to drive your plot.

Here's what's exciting. Your word count doesn't explode when adding in a few small details, but when you use those adjectives, you immerse your readers into the setting right away, pulling them in and making them experience just what your characters are. But there's a little more to consider as well when thinking about the setting.

Create Mood and Atmosphere

It's important for the setting to immediately establish the mood of the moment. That's a crucial thing for engaging your reader. Since they are walking in just that moment, they need to feel as though they are there, and that includes the feel of the room, as it were. At a party? Everyone dancing or giggling has a very different vibe than people standing around awkwardly. The music choice, food on a buffet table, and the clothes are all clues to the atmosphere. A party with everyone in evening wear will be quite different from shrieking kids and a clown making balloon animals.

Since every word counts in order to be in your desired length category for sales, here are some tips for mood and atmosphere.

- **Be Selective with Details:** Choose only the details that reinforce the desired mood of that setting. If it's a hot, muggy day, describe the suffocating air, the dampness that seeps into clothes. If it's one of those "everything is going right" moments, maybe you'll point out the sunshine, the gentle breeze, the happy sound of children at the playground. All small things, but ones that contribute to your setting.

- **Sensory Details:** Use a few carefully chosen details from the five senses (smell, sound, touch, sight, taste) to make the location feel real and immediately immerse the reader. This is much more effective than a long visual description and places the reader right there in the book.

Unless that's what your subgenre calls for, like Regency romances, your goal isn't to be over the top with your details. It's not to drown your readers in three pages describing the field of flowers or the dress she's wearing that shimmers like moonlight. Nope. A few words and move on. In short romance especially, restraint is key. It's important to be succinct with your words because there's so much more to write.

Do you remember how I also said that the setting could be used to help with the conflict? Here's a little more on that.

A Setting's Connection to Characters and Conflicts

Your setting must serve your story. This bears repeating, but I'll just wait and let you reread the sentence. Go ahead.

Ready to move on? Let's do it.

Why is it so important the setting must serve the story? Think of your setting as almost another character. It's such a critical part of making your story believable, it's going to contribute to influencing your character's reactions and decisions, and it's also going to add that conflict I mentioned earlier. Here's how.

- **Influence on Character:** Your setting is the perfect way to mirror your character's feelings, and thoughts, and actions. If your character is feeling lonely, they might be in an empty, quiet house, something that is echoing how they feel internally. You could also use your setting as a contrast to how your character is feeling. If they are depressed, maybe they are in a cheerful crowd, arms crossed, shoulders slumped. The same can go with your character's actions. Are they running, while everyone else seems to be standing still? Are they sitting on a bench, watching everyone speed past?

- **Generate Conflict:** Let's finally get to how the setting can cause a conflict. There are two ways this can happen, either through external conflict, like a storm keeping your character from going somewhere, or with internal conflict, like being afraid to do something because the town gossip is right there watching every move your character makes.

Here's a quick lesson on the types of external and internal conflicts. External conflicts include:

- **Person versus Person**

  - This is the most common form of external conflict, where the protagonist is pitted against an antagonist or another character.

- **Person versus Nature**

  - This type of conflict involves a character struggling against forces of nature, such as weather events, the environment, or wild animals.

- **Person versus Society**

- Here, we have a character going against the rules, laws, traditions, or values of a group or government. That includes expectations from parents, friends, and employers.

Internal conflicts aren't broken down into types, because internal (also called indirect) conflicts are those that take place within a character's own mind. This is often called Character versus Self. It's internal or indirect because the struggle is not against an observable external force, like another person or a storm or a financial problem, but instead, they are having a mental or emotional battle.

That would include something like the morals they grew up with, their core beliefs. A deeply personal thought that influences the character's actions and decisions in the external plot. This could be the character in a situation where they are asked to lie or to steal, when it goes against their personal belief system. It doesn't matter if the lie would hurt or help someone, it goes against what they stand for, and makes them war with themselves over the decision.

This could also be where that feeling of unworthiness or of shame or fear around something keeps them from achieving their goal. Embarrassment is a type of shame, and any of those feelings of unworthiness or fear can come from the past or the present.

The setting can put your character into these conflicts, forcing them to have to choose what to do, while struggling against what they or what others want.

The most important thing to remember about your setting is it shouldn't just be there, hanging out in the background like a static image your characters are just dropped into. It should feel real and be a critical part of the story. Your setting exists to shape your world and your characters, and how they act or react.

But what about picking a location? Choosing the perfect setting in your short fiction is something that I've had others tell me stresses them out. How can they find the perfect romantic place, set up that moment, and bring their couple together (or apart!) using those setting details?

When it comes to creating a scene, you are limited only by your imagination. Even the most mundane of things can be romantic or chaotic, if done right. Here's what I mean.

A beach is a pretty popular spot for romance. But what could happen at the beach to draw your couple into a romantic, an awkward, or even a conflict situation? What about a sudden storm, where they need to seek shelter? Getting dragged out by a wave. A dog running loose and snarling (or wagging its tail) at one of your characters. Someone playing some music, and an offer to dance beneath the stars. Running into someone they've not seen for a while, or wish they hadn't gotten spotted by.

Once you think about where you'd like your character to be, you can create multiple what-if's that could happen to push them together, keep them together, or pull them apart.

For those days you are feeling stuck, turn to the back of the book for a list I have for you with loads of settings to get your ideas sparking.

Remember that time of day can play heavily into your setting as well. Some things are scarier at night or more beautiful. Play around with seasons too. Fall or winter might push your chilly couple together, while spring or summer encourages an outing.

All right. You've learned about characters, and about the setting. Let's get into the other elements you need to craft the perfect story.

THE PERFECT MEET-CUTE

Ahhh! The meet-cute! Once upon this baby writer's time, I wondered...why the heck is it called that? If you don't know either, thank goodness it wasn't just me! Here's the simple explanation. Meet-cute (and sometimes you'll see it without the hyphen, like this: meet cute) means the meeting that's in a cute way.

As I typed that out, I sort of imagined her tripping and him catching her and all the little glittery sparkles floating around them as they lock eyes and know *this is it*. And, that's sort of what you want to have. But in a (are you sick of me saying it?!) believable way.

In short romance, your meet-cute should happen early—ideally in the first 10–15% of your story. In a

5,000-word story, that means in the first 500–750 words. In a 20,000-word novella, you'll want that within the first 2,000–3,000 words. An exception could be if you are writing dual POV, alternating chapters, and you choose to have them meet in Chapter 3, which might be closer to 4,000 words.

While I'm going to leave the how it happens up to you, the meet-cute is one of those wonderful moments limited only by your imagination. It's also the most critical scene in your story. After all, that's how your couple meet each other or, if they already knew each other in the friend/coworker zone, that's how they have that sparkle, glitter, *this is it* moment. No pressure, right? In friends to lovers or second chance romance, the meet-cute is really what could be called a *re-meeting* or *seeing them differently moment*—but it serves the same purpose.

An important thing about the meet-cute is that it needs to be memorable. After all, wouldn't it be boring if Jack and Jill were just on their phones and totally ignoring each other as they crossed the street? Where's the story going to go? Not very far! There's no amusing or awkward or unusual thing that makes them lock eyes and the glittery sparkles fall. There's no conflict or sparks either good or bad.

So, it's got to be memorable. Let's have Jill on her phone and Jack just has put his away. They are crossing the street in opposite directions when a car runs the light! Jack sees it coming, yanks her out of the way just in time, pulling her into his arms, and they lock eyes. Glittery sparkles!

(And, yeah, this is a thinly disguised warning: don't be on your phone while crossing traffic because there might not be a hot guy to save you.)

Much more memorable, eh? We've served our purpose of the meet-cute, we got our couple together, and we've also done it in a memorable way.

The connection between your characters doesn't have to be instantly positive. In fact, an immediate conflict or tension between them often provides the most engaging spark and reveals character. That can be done in a few ways.

Opposites Attract: Have you heard that phrase before? When your characters instantly clash or have opposing goals (competing for the same job, being on opposite sides in a dispute, etc.) it creates an immediate, engaging reaction. Even better, it makes the reader wonder if your characters will ever get together because they are just so different!

A Problematic Encounter: This is a fun one! Spilling coffee on her new boss's white shirt, bumping into someone while not paying attention, getting stuck in a tree trying to rescue a stray kitten, or even some sort of a takeout order mix-up can start with initial irritation for one or both of your characters, and end with an HEA or HFN.

Forced Proximity: This is such a popular trope. Put your characters in a situation they can't easily escape from (snowed in, trapped in a car, locked in a room, etc.) and force them to be stuck so they *have* to communicate with each other, even if they are not wanting to.

But did you know that you also can use your meet-cute to do a bit of the work in revealing more about your character? Since you only have so many words you can use in your short fiction, why not make them do double duty? Can you create an interaction that shows a quick glimpse into who the character is? Maybe a quirk or something they value?

A Shared Unique Circumstance: Same last name, went to the same Pre-K, also like their soda with lemon, whatever. If your couple has some sort of thing that not many other people share, that might be the makings of a romance! There could even be a shared fear, and one that's not super common. For example, they dislike open concept ceilings with all the pipes out, because what if they burst? It doesn't have to be a huge fear; it doesn't even have to be founded. It just has to be there.

An Unlikely Hero or Heroine: Sometimes, it's just a small action we do that has a larger impact. It's true in real life and it could be true in your story as well. Anything from a pet rescue to finding a lost bracelet or dropping a dime in the parking meter when someone ran out of time. It doesn't have to be a big thing, unless you want it to be, but a small moment that shows how thoughtful your character is might just make for the perfect introduction to them, and a great meet-cute.

Shared Passions: Maybe they bump into each other while staring at the same painting at a gallery. They reach for the same book at the used bookstore. It could be anything, but already having that common ground, and that shared interest, makes for a great way to both meet, and set up a scene.

But let's not forget you need just a little bit more than an action to set off that meet-cute. You also need a little dialogue, a setting. Remember Jack and Jill? What if he'd saved her life, then righted her on her feet, and kept on crossing the street? Where's our romance? It would make for some confusing reading, wouldn't it? After all, it seems that romance isn't going anywhere.

What's your writing strength? Is it clever dialogue? Crafting beautiful scenery? The dialogue exchange and the environment your characters are in are crucial for adding to your story. How best to do that? That's going to be up to you and your story, but here are a few suggestions.

Clever Banter: The right words can really give your characters chemistry, and also show their personalities. Your characters don't have to be obvious about liking the other. In fact, it's more fun when they hint around it at first, and we get that whole awkward, shy thing. Or the: I hate you vibe. Regardless of which way you go, that meet-cute needs to have your characters avoid what they *really* want to say, letting you build that delicious tension.

Unexpected Settings: Let me preface this by saying there is nothing wrong with choosing a common setting for your meet-cute. Not. A. Thing. But, if you don't want to be like everyone else, or if you've written a zillion books and are running out of places to have them meet that won't drive you crazy, how about some outside-the-box ideas? Choosing an unconventional location (a yoga retreat, a political rally, a gamer's convention, an auction) adds an element of the unexpected and helps the scene stand out. It also might be really fun to write, if it's something you'd never do yourself.

Mistaken Identity: Yes, this is a trope. Great job noticing! But it's also a great meet-cute when it's done as one. For example, one character mistakes the other for someone else (a blind date, a celebrity, someone who works at the store). Depending on your character's personality, this could lead to some super comedic or awkward interactions that eventually turn into a memorable introduction. And, that HEA. Cue the sparkly glitter!

While your meet-cute needs to match your book and your plot, obviously, there's nothing wrong with having some fun with it. This is a chance to make your story, no matter how large or small in word count, an opportunity for a memorable moment that's going to bring your couple together in a sweet way.

A word of caution before we move on about meet-cute clichés. While tropes are great, some meet-cutes are so overdone they've become eye-roll inducing, like the bumping into someone and spilling coffee I mentioned earlier. If you are going to do a meet-cute that's common, make it fresh. Add some unexpected details or a reaction the reader wouldn't expect, like how the character looks down, shrugs, and says, "I didn't like that shirt anyway." Make it a milkshake, have it land on the shoes or the backpack, or something different from the white shirt.

Whatever you choose to do, make it your own, and make it original, and...make it believable. Now, it's time to talk about the emotional stakes. Ready to move on?

ESCALATING THE EMOTIONAL STAKES

Emotional stakes and conflicts are the things I love to write most. That's why they are each getting their own chapter! Be warned, this one is a little long—but emotional stakes are what make readers fall in love with your characters, so it's worth spending time on.

Emotion is important in your book so that you can connect your characters with your readers, and there are several ways you can do that. Sometimes the emotional stakes are those that come from the relationship. Other times, it's the setting or scene. Regardless, there are some great ways to ramp up the emotional tension that I can't wait to share with you. But first, let's talk about why it's so important to have it.

If you've ever put a book down, I bet it was because it didn't hold your interest. Chances are really good you didn't connect with the characters. They were too generic. Flat. They were fine, right? But boring. You just couldn't feel sympathetic or angry or any sort of pull or desire toward them. For the story, there was no conflict, no thing that made you worry or wonder what was going to happen.

What was missing was an emotional connection. The biggest challenge in writing short romance is that you must convince the reader that the characters are truly in love, not just attracted to each other. The speed of the romance means you have to use literary shortcuts to convey instant compatibility. We just don't have time to draw it out.

For just a moment, think about some of your favorite characters from books or movies or shows. I'm betting some of those you've not enjoyed for years. Maybe, if you are like me, decades. But...you still remember how that book made you feel. How hard you rooted for that character. How you sobbed through a few chapters, used a half box of tissues, and were emotionally crushed for days afterward.

Do you remember? Are you feeling that now as you think about it? That's because the author wrote a character that you connected to emotionally. You felt them. You were right there. That was done both because of who they were and what was happening to them.

In a movie or show, music swells in the background, or plays mournfully to show us emotional scenes. In a book, we have to make that happen with our words. But how can that be done when the word count is small?

We've talked already about creating your character, and we've also talked about setting the scene and the meet-cute. Those all need emotional connections. Let's delve a little deeper into the topic, though.

What makes you instantly connect with someone? I'm guessing the answer is learning more about them. It's easy to feel sympathetic toward someone who is grieving or going through a loss or traumatic incident. It's also easy to feel righteous indignation for them when someone betrays or hurts them.

If you were to pick up a book in the store, and on the very first page the woman is thinking about how scared she is of dogs, but she's going to be the best darn dog walker possible for the old lady who gave her a chance because she needs the job to pay for her mom's hospital bills, you'll want to keep reading, right? Especially if right after she thinks that, something spooks the little pup and it breaks free.

Oh yeah, you are going to turn that page, right? Not only are you feeling bad for the woman who is trying so hard to conquer her fear to make money to help her mom...but you are going to want to see what happens to the dog! Does she catch it? Does it get lost and she gets in more trouble? Does it lead to one heck of a meet-cute? (That's my vote!)

The point is, that was an emotional opening. You had a connection with the character. You connected with the conflict. You want to know what happens. You are also hoping that she's going to be okay, her mom will be okay, and the dog will be okay.

That sure is a lot of stuff happening in just a short little thing you could write on a single page. It could be done, too, with a single mom, a woman lost in the city, a broken down car. By putting some emotional connection in there based on a negative emotion (fear, guilt, panic, loss, anger, etc.) you draw the reader in wanting to know what happens.

The same can be done with positive emotions. However, in order to create an emotional connection, if you want to have a positive emotion at the start of your book, you're going to need to tack on a negative one.

This does bleed into conflict, but they are slightly different things, so let's keep going. Why do we need to throw in something bad when she's on top of the world?

Because no one wants to read about someone whose life is all sunshine and roses. They just don't. We need some suffering. We need that angst. The unrequited love. The never going to trust a guy again. Something to connect us because, let's be honest...we've all had those feelings far more than we've had blue skies and rainbows.

And...there is nothing more satisfying for a reader than when the bad things work out and the main character gets far more than they hoped for.

That satisfaction is made possible by the emotional connection. Let's talk about some of the ways that can happen.

Instant Vulnerability

In real life, vulnerability is built over time. In a bite-sized romance, you must compress this process into the first few scenes. Let's head back to the dog walker story. Remember what's going on in her life? Sharing backstories, especially those with vulnerabilities (her fears and her need) helps create that reader-character connection. When that meet-cute happens, this is also how you are going to show that your characters are meant for each other. It could be fated mates, it could be sensing a kindred spirit, it could be opposites attract, or a hero. Whatever it is, it happens, and they just know the missing puzzle piece is now there.

Shared Confidences

Remember, every word counts, so don't be boring. Don't waste space with fluff that doesn't need to be there. Instead of talking about the weather, force your characters to share something deeply personal right away. (I lost the dog I was walking! I have to have this job. My mom is really sick and I need to get her medicine.) Even in real life, we feel a connection with someone when we are facing a crisis or are in a forced proximity scenario.

Here's another example. Say your female character goes into a coffee shop, and just stares blankly at the menu board. The guy taking her order says, "Rough day?" Before she knows it, she's admitted that, yeah it is, and tells him what happened. Instead of him just telling her, "Gee, that sucks. Hope tomorrow is better," he says something like, "You know, last year the same thing happened to me." That opens up a shared connection between the two of them.

I See You Moment

Cliché? Maybe, but we all love it when one character sees past the other's facade or social mask. We do. When we get to see the jerk help a small child, drop off a bag of canned goods at the food pantry, pump the gas in an old woman's car, we get a little pitter-patter and go aww! When we see the shy wallflower who's getting teased because no one will dance with her lock eyes with someone across the room, and time stands still, oh yeah! We know something good is going to happen.

This interaction, be it one-sided (watching the jerk) or where both parties experience that moment of seeing (the wallflower) allows the protagonist (and the reader) to skip the surface layer of connection that takes pages and pages to build and connect immediately to the love interest's very being.

This works because it creates instant intimacy—the character (and reader) feels they've glimpsed the real person beneath the surface, which in real life might take months to discover.

Clean Intimacy and Physical Tension

This is a book about writing clean, yeah? So, how can you make your readers feel invested in the relationship between your characters when you aren't going to have any on-page physical activity beyond kisses only? In clean romance, the intensity of the physical connection must be channeled into emotional tension and sensory details. The goal is to make a simple touch feel like an electric, seismic event. We aren't overexaggerating like a cartoon character with awooga eyes, but we are making it feel like nothing they've ever felt. What we are doing is heightening the senses.

Writing attraction and desire, but keeping it clean, is absolutely possible. You can build that tension and keep it ramped up all day long if you apply the proper techniques. While practice makes perfect, here are some suggestions.

When describing the physical closeness of your couple, focus on non-visual, non-sexual sensory information. Remember the five senses we talked about earlier? We're going to use some of them. This means you are not going to be surface level with sentences like: Her blue eyes were bright. He was so hot I couldn't believe it. She had bright red hair. He was so tall. Nope. That's not going to build an emotional connection. Here's what will: those adjectives we also talked about.

- **Scent:** The specific smell of their clothing, hair, or cologne. (She smelled like vanilla, he had a spicy scent, there was a unique scent all their own, that made them want to draw closer.)

- **Sound:** The steady rhythm of their breathing, their heart thumping loudly, the warm chuckle, the whimper of fear, the distant sound of a siren or a dog barking.

- **Temperature/Touch:** The warmth radiating from their skin, a calloused hand, silky hair, a smooth shirt, a prickly beard, chills from one's touch, the tickling sensation of a whisper.

Proximity

Using forced or prolonged proximity can maximize tension without physical contact. This tension could be the good kind, longing for the other, or it could be just as delicious with the anger and the enemies to lovers trope. What happens when your characters are stuck in a small car? Pressed together in a crowded elevator? Forced to share the same room when their car breaks down in the middle of nowhere with a nearly full hotel? Throw in some of those sensory details of how they smell or feel. The proximity should become agonizingly close, making their shared desire to be closer obvious, but unobtainable.

Intentional Touch

Since writing clean romance means that physical affection is reserved, what you do put on page should be highly meaningful. This creates an emotional payoff, and becomes the satisfying moment a reader craves. It's also serving as a glimpse into what the characters are really feeling and wanting.

Every single touch—fingers brushing, moving hair out of someone's face, a prolonged handshake, hand on the small of the back, the first kiss—no matter what it is, it must be a progression of the story. It should also feel like a level up in their romance.

It's okay to have the fingers brush and the sparks happen on page three, but that intimate hand on the lower back or the protective arm around the shoulder ought to happen after something that drew them closer together. Maybe the vulnerable verbal moment, a physical scare, a shy look at the need for physical contact.

Common Goals

What better way to both draw our couple together and bring some emotion into the story than to work toward a common goal? Remember the dog walker story at the start of the chapter? The pup has run off, and our heroine has got to find it. Not only will the woman who owns her be devastated, but our heroine needs the job. She also needs to prove to herself she can do this. Cue that meet-cute, and imagine she's met a guy who will help her look. That's the two of them being pushed together for this goal of finding Fido.

You'll want to keep reading, even if you are more of a cat lover than a dog fan, simply because by now, you're worried. Can she find it? Will she be able to face her fears? And what about the guy? What kind of person is he? Can they work together? Or is he really a jerk?

If you were writing this story, it would differ from if I were, and that's part of what makes this so exciting. It doesn't matter where you take it. By focusing on those negative emotions, and hinting at the positive ones (a resolution, the guy saving the day) you've got your reader emotionally invested.

Conflict

We are about to have a whole chapter on this, but I want to jump in really quick to say nothing gets a reader invested in a story like a little conflict. We all want to know if the hero will save the day in time. If the girl she sees him walking with is his new girlfriend. If the person who has given up on love will have a second chance at it.

Conflict, internal or external, is a huge part of your emotional connection. It can be anything from *I want to talk to her, but I am scared*, to *I want to help her, but she's locked in a tower by an evil wizard and I'm not sure how.*

Distraction

This is one of the most important tools in your emotional toolbox. Build up that glorious tension. The whole I have to touch you, have to kiss you. The things are about to happen, and what are we going to do? Bring them closer, get them right there...and then don't let it happen. Distract the couple.

About to kiss? Someone walks in. The phone rings. A stray dog barks. Their hands tentatively reach toward the other? Someone they know says hello. They see their ex. A guy walking past bumps them. He knocks over his drink. About to put an arm around her? She drops something. A bee stings her.

Whatever it is, make it happen right at the point they are finally, finally going to have that first meaningful touch. It will give your characters so much internal emotion (irritation, disappointment, sadness, jealousy) and help to build conflict. The trick, though, is not to overuse it, so that you don't frustrate your reader.

Dialogue: Dos and Don'ts for Emotion

Remember...with only so many words allowed, you've got to get to the heart of your story quickly. That connection needs to happen very fast, if not instantly in your story, but you've also got to keep things moving. There's no time at all to slow down the story with your dialogue in short romance.

While using small talk dialogue to slow down a high-tension point in longer fiction while building it up is a wonderful tool, it's also something that some readers put in even when there's nothing happening in the scene, thinking that it's needed. Have you ever read (or skipped over?) someone doing word for word a morning bathroom routine? Leaving somewhere with all the goodbyes to every person they pass by? Discussing the weather with a stranger? It's boring. It doesn't serve the story.

There is an exception, and that is that small talk CAN work in short romance if:

- It reveals something about a character (She asks his favorite ride at the fair, and he admits they make him sick)

- It creates contrast (a happy surface conversation while internal thoughts are showing panic)

- It shows awkwardness that's endearing (stammering, saying things that come out weird)

Small talk for the sake of small talk slows your story to a crawl. But if it reveals character, creates tension, or shows personality? Then it can work. Use it strategically, and make conversations that connect your couple.

The majority of your couple's conversation needs to either advance the story's plot (applicable the most in novella lengths) or the emotional connection between them.

But wait, you might be saying. Everyone engages in small talk. The get to know you questions. Maybe I'm in the minority, that I hate those myself. Perhaps that's why I adore short romance. Yes, everyone does, but that's when you can tell, not show. *The next half hour, they traded those get to know you questions everyone has.* Or: *After he said goodbye to everyone in the office...*

Done. That's all you needed. The justification for skipping the small talk is that your couple is so perfectly matched, they bypass needing the typical social fillers, which includes small talk.

Though not dialogue, the same goes for your character's actions. It's enough to say they got out of bed, dug through the closet, and got ready for work. We don't need to know they brushed their teeth, put on deodorant, combed their hair. It doesn't build any sort of emotional connection or escalate it. It doesn't increase the conflict that helps you work toward the HEA or HFA. It's just extra.

Conflict deserves its own deep dive, so let's move on to Chapter 11 where we'll explore it fully.

Creating Conflict

In short romance, because the connection is so immediate, the conflict in your story can't just be about whether your couple *likes* each other, but about whether they can *sustain* that initial spark. Without the promise to the reader that there is going to be a HEA, your book falls into the concept of lusting, not something lasting. There's no love, no set future. Conflict is proof that their instant connection is strong enough to last.

Why? Well, if your characters waltz effortlessly to their happily ever after, the story will feel flat and the romance will seem superficial. Nothing was earned. There was no struggle that brought them together, overcame a fear, or warmed the heart. Don't we all feel moved when the person or couple overcomes something difficult to get their reward, that thing that means more to them than anything else?

Conflicts (because you can put more than one in your book) test the characters and force them to actively choose each other and the thing that will make them as a person grow.

Sometimes, the instant connection between a couple gets an eye roll. Remember early on I talked about how this needed to be believable? Conflict is one of the things that will make your couple's romance feel earned, the story linger in your reader's mind, and then give an incredible buildup to the moment they get together.

Conflict is also the proof that your couple are meant to be together, and that the spark of *this is the one* they had initially will last. They are proving to themselves and to the readers that they aren't just in love with the idea of love, but they are in love with each other.

While you've likely heard about story beats, even for short romance, those of you who are pantsers, like me, may cringe at the idea. Don't worry. I'm not about to lecture about what goes before what. In fact, I'm going to simplify the whole concept for you.

Whether it's a super short 3,000 words or a longer 30,000 words, conflict is used the same in a story. There are two parts (see? Simplifying!) to it. First, establishing what's at risk and the second, what might take it away.

The conflict can be related to your main plot if you have the space for the words, or it can be related to the couple. You can even have more than one conflict if you have the available word count.

For example, you could have her problem, his problem, and their problem. A historical I wrote, *Mail-Order Teacher,* is a perfect example. He arrives to town, expecting to solve the truancy issue at the school he's been hired at and teach the students with an iron fist. However, there was a mix-up...and a much older woman thinks he's there to marry her.

On the other side of town, our female main character is recently widowed, and has been fending off unwanted advances from someone. To complicate things, the man she'd married hadn't been a love match but one of necessity. She needed a home and he needed a mother for his children. Who are now hers, and one of whom has been skipping school and trying to find work because they are trying to survive.

Do you see what we have there? His conflict, her conflict. And the conflict is going to bring them together into a joint conflict because much more happens. However, the conflict is used to help him grow as a person, her grow as a person, and pushes them together to grow them as a couple.

If it weren't for the conflict in a story, there wouldn't be the emotional payoff that your reader needs when the couple finally comes together.

Let me say that again. The emotional payoff is a need. If you want your readers to return to you, they need to feel all the feels. Good, bad, edge-of-the-seat anxious, or ugly crying.

You know how we broke down what conflict is into two simple things? Establishing what's at risk and what might take it away? We're going to do the same with types of conflict. Each can be and should be used differently and at different points in your story.

One thing you might be wondering about is when to introduce conflict. In short romance, you might introduce external conflict early (they're competing for the same job) while internal conflict deepens as they get closer (his fear of commitment surfaces just as she's falling for him). The key is escalation—conflicts should get more intense, not easier, until the climax.

Let's start first with internal conflict, the thing that many, many authors forget about, but holds such a key to making your story unforgettable.

Internal Conflict

Internal conflict arises from thoughts, emotions, and the way that we try to cope with them. The loss of someone or something, real or perceived, and the reaction your mind or body has is an internal conflict. The feeling exhausted, but knowing you really need to get up and do something and beating yourself up for it, even as you can hardly keep your eyes open is an internal conflict. So is worrying if someone likes you, the spiraling thoughts of having seen something suspicious, and so is that feeling of wondering if something is too good to be true.

We all have internal conflicts; however, not everyone can tell. On the page, since we don't have mood music setting the scene, we need to be descriptive with our words. It's very important to paint that picture for our readers of someone's internal conflict in a realistic way. This is where you'll put in physical actions (pacing, tossing and turning, slumped shoulders) alongside the warring or restless or sabotaging thoughts going on in your reader's mind.

In clean short romance, external conflicts (like family feuds or natural disasters) are often present, but internal conflict is paramount to creating that emotional connection with your reader. Since the hero and heroine are usually perfect for each other thanks to that hand tingle or jolt to the stomach when they locked eyes, they are going to need the conflict in your story to keep your reader turning the pages.

When it comes to internal conflict, the biggest obstacle should be the emotional wounds your individuals bring to the relationship. It's these emotional wounds (the thoughts, emotions, and the way that your characters try to cope with them) that give that satisfying ending when your couple finally gets together.

Internal conflict usually comes down to: "I don't believe I deserve _______ because _______." That can be done by your character having a fear of commitment from a past trauma or fear of abandonment, and the speed of their connection is making them unsettled, wondering if this is all too good to be true and if it will last. It could also be your character feeling unworthy of affection from the other, when they feel that person is too good for them or they have a secret they are terrified of anyone finding out because it makes them seem less than.

That secret doesn't even have to be anything huge, like they've been pretending to be someone they aren't. It could be a smaller, everyday sort of thing like debt or a past mistake, or an illness or physical disability.

Here's an example from one of my own books, *A Sleigh Ride for Charlotte*, showing the internal conflict. I'll put it in italics, so you can see when the excerpt is over.

"I'm not who she wants. It's him, not me," he suddenly burst out, pacing. All of his hurt, all of his insecurities and fears and upset rushed out of him. Now that the flood had started, he couldn't hold it back.

"I'm not rich, I'm not handsome. I have nothing to offer. A doctor with his first practice—a new one at that—in a small town is not wealthy. Why, half of my patients don't

pay me in coin, but in service or food. I couldn't give her all she deserves."

"What does she deserve?" Charlotte's mother asked, placing her hands in her lap, while her eyes never left his.

"She deserves someone who loves her. Who can give her what she desires. Who can care for her and protect her and...and I am none of those things."

There, we see all those worries and insecurities, all that internal anguish. It makes the reader want to keep going, to find out what happens, and it resonates with them as well. They now understand why he doesn't feel like he deserves her. Haven't we all felt like we weren't good enough for something or someone or to be included? This is the foundation of many romance internal conflicts. *I don't believe I deserve _____ because_____.* Write it down. Post it on your wall. This simple framework will help you craft believable emotional wounds every time.

Quite honestly, it doesn't matter what the thing is that is causing them to feel as though they are undeserving of love or that person, just that they have one.

External Conflicts

External conflicts are things that happen to your character. No phone in sight in an emergency, an animal bite, a storm, being left at the altar, running into an ex, being late for work, falling off a horse. Those are all external conflicts. There's something happening, and it is happening to your character.

Logistical or moral roadblocks are fantastic conflict options to have for bite-sized romance. They don't take long to set up, can be resolved within your word count, and in the case of using a moral roadblock, there's so much conflict and tension it can create internally, and really give your reader that emotional connection.

Let me pause. Do you notice I keep using some of the same words over and over? Conflict, emotional connection, realistic/believable, tension? It's because those are such important things to have in your story. Without them, you quite possibly could still have a quick, fun read. But it won't be memorable. It won't make readers one-click buy your next book.

That's our goal outside of writing just to write, right? We want to make enough money to pay for the production costs of the next book, and to have some to set aside for our other needs.

So, what are some of the external conflicts that could serve to keep your characters apart yet force them together to show everyone they were meant for each other? There's quite a list, really, but what you'll want is something that either falls under logistics (you might also think of this as a situational conflict) or a misunderstanding of something that goes against your main character's core values.

Let's start with logistics. Scheduling woes and distance troubles are all logistics-based. It's something that's going to cause your characters to have to figure out a solution to the problem, and often together. Other ideas could be a boss/employee situation, a disapproving family, social status, or the fact they have no idea what the other looks like. These situations might force your characters to sneak around, adding tension and stakes.

Something else that's great at adding an external conflict is the misunderstanding of another's core values. If something is important to one character, but another brushes it off as not really important, your first character might feel that's a betrayal. We could use a cultural difference, for example, or a social one. Maybe she's dedicated to environmental activism and he just accepted a job with an oil company. Or he values honesty above all else, but she's been hiding her real identity because she witnessed a crime. These conflicts cut deeper than logistics—they challenge whether the relationship can even work. There's a conflict in that what's important to her doesn't seem important to him (or vice versa).

And...think on that for a second. Is there anything more realistic than that kind of conflict? What's important to one person doesn't seem important to another? I suspect you see that, maybe even live that, frequently.

This sort of conflict is a communication type. It's best solved by being honest, and open, and vulnerable. Those can also be conflicts, if showing emotions is difficult for that character or if they feel like there's a very good reason why they shouldn't be honest. But this also leads to a great resolution, and emotional growth for the character and an emotional connection for the reader, as the character chooses to have trust over their doubts.

When it comes to internal or external conflicts, there's really no limit on what you can write. Anything that causes your couple to get defensive, upset, hurt, scared, or any of the other emotions we humans feel, can work wonderfully.

In the back of the book, I've included a huge list of internal and external conflicts for you. Mix and match or let them inspire you! You can even add your own because it is not an all-inclusive list. Whatever you imagine, you can create the perfect story out of.

Of course, creating conflict is only half the battle. The resolution—how your characters overcome these obstacles and choose each other—is what delivers that satisfying HEA. But before we get there, we need to understand the journey between conflict and resolution, which we'll explore in the next chapter.

GRAND GESTURES AND RESOLUTIONS

While conflict can be woven throughout your book in small or large ways, there really is only one "grand gesture" moment in your book. This is the thing that helps with the resolution of your story, bringing the couple through their conflict, and allowing that happily ever after or happy for now ending.

This moment happens shortly after the conflict. Maybe you've heard of the all is lost moment? This is the moment when the conflict has gotten to be so big that your character(s) feels like giving up. That's going to be around 75% or so into your story.

If you are anything like me, and don't care for math, let me give you a rough idea of where that might fall for you. In a 5,000-word story, that's around 3,750 words in. For 15,000 words, it's around 11,250. A 25,000-word novella, it's around 18,750 words. Adjust that for the length you are writing, but the principle stays the same—it happens near the end, but not at the end.

This is the point when it feels like, well, all is lost! There's no hope. Not for them, not for the relationship. That is also the point in your story where only something big will bring them together. The grand gesture.

Let me walk you through the typical expectations for your grand gesture and resolution. Keep in mind that your allotted word count is going to dictate how much page space you give this section. Can it all happen over a few hundred words? Absolutely! It could also happen over a few chapters.

Ready to craft what happens after the conflict has been created?

First, there's a *collision*. This is where the internal and the external conflicts clash, leading to a temporary split in the couple's relationship. For example, someone terrified of being left behind pushes their partner away when they get a job offer states away—creating a self-fulfilling prophecy born of fear.

The key here is readers need to see it coming. They need to know that it's terrible and awful, but it's for the character's own good to go through this, and something much better is waiting for them on the other side. If they can just get there.

A simple argument, a hint of jealousy, that's not enough. It's not going to make a grand gesture or a resolution feel big enough for your reader, so avoid a small clash. Use those as little conflicts earlier on. This needs to be the relationship-is-dying kind of conflict.

The next thing that happens is the *realization*. Internal dialogue or emotions are wonderful at showing this. Your character is going to realize that the initial spark they felt wasn't a mistake and it wasn't a fluke. It was real, and worth taking a chance for. They go from: *This is a bad idea*, to *I want to try and make this work*.

Your character realizes that they are about to lose something special, possibly something they'll never have again, and it might just be worth the risk to step out of their comfort zone in order to chase after it. The conflict and the result of that conflict pushed them to this feeling, and this point is where we see character growth.

Afterward, we've finally got that grand gesture! That moment where your character performs a visible action (that's their grand gesture) to overcome the conflict and prove to themselves and the one they love (and the reader!) that this connection is real, and it's solid, and it will last forever.

The grand gesture has to be grand. That means huge. Big. It can't just be flowers and an "I'm sorry." Let's go to that example from a moment ago, someone pushing the other away when the second person has a job opportunity a few states away. What would be a grand gesture by a person who is scared of being abandoned?

Let's brainstorm together. Maybe they start looking for a job in that area too, or an apartment. Maybe they even quit their current job (even better, one they love, to show they love their partner more) or maybe, they show up with a suitcase the day the other is going to drive off, and say "take me with you."

The whole point of this grand gesture is to show the one they love that they are the most important thing in the world to them. The love is bigger than their fears and doubts and all of the scary emotions that come with being human.

And, this is super important for the reader to experience too. Don't gloss over it. This is one of the most satisfying things for a reader to experience, especially when you are writing clean romance because you aren't giving them those physically intimate scenes as the relationship progresses. Instead, this emotional connection serves as a physical connection, and one that your reader (and your characters) need.

But there's another piece still to this, and it's the *consequence*. So, your guy is standing there, suitcase in hand. "Take me with you!" he's begging. But...will she? Should she? Can she trust that he's not going to be a jerk? That he's not just playing her?

The consequence of their previous actions from that conflict is a moment for both of them, but especially for one of them, to think, to wonder, "Hmmm. Should I take them back? Could we work things out? Are we really meant to be together?"

Again, don't rush this. Let that character show some hesitation, some reluctance. After all, think back to all those iconic parts in movies and TV shows, when someone comes running after another person in the rain, and it's dripping down their nose as they are begging. Does the person being begged for forgiveness immediately say, "I love you, I forgive you?"

Of course not! It's drawn out. They are thinking. Considering. Weighing their options. Should they? Or is it better to move on? Could this potentially happen again? Is it worth the risk?

This is one of those points where your reader needs to be on the edge of their seat. It doesn't matter that they likely know the couple will get together at the end of the story. Does. Not. Matter. The not knowing, the hesitation, that's what creates tension, that's what creates the emotional impact, and that's what keeps the character-reader connection strong.

Your reader is pulling for them, hoping that it will work out...but that hesitation...that having to think it over...it creates doubt. (And more conflict! Imagine I'm singing that word. Make it two fluttery syllables. Con-fliccctttt. That's how important this tool is to have in your book.)

Show the fear, the unease, the hesitation. Even though the gesture is a grand one, one of your characters still has to choose. In short romance, this moment of hesitation might be a few paragraphs or a page—just long enough to make readers hold their breath, but not so long you pad your word count unnecessarily.

But...sometimes, both characters need to make a grand gesture—he quits his job to follow her, AND she turns down the promotion to stay near his sick parent. This works beautifully when both have been wrong or both need to show growth.

A perfect example of a grand gesture proving love is in the short story of *The Gift of the Maji* by O. Henry. If you aren't familiar with it, the general premise is the husband and wife loved each other so much, they were willing to sacrifice their all to bring joy to the other, not realizing that what they gave up affected the other's gift.

Now, a word of warning, since you are writing bite-sized fiction, and it's possible it's taking place over a short period of time. It is critical to make sure your grand gesture is proportional to your story's timeline. If your couple has known each other just a few days, the gesture should be meaningful but not life-destroying. If it's been a few months, bigger sacrifices (like a move or job change) become more believable.

However, it's important to remember that not every resolution needs a Romeo-outside-the-window moment or the sacrifices made in *The Gift of the Maji*. Sometimes the grand gesture is only internal—choosing vulnerability, saying I love you first, or simply showing up. The *grand* part is about emotional significance, not always dramatic action.

Okay! Fast forward. We've drawn that out long enough, and there's much more for you to get through on your short romance writing journey. Crazy how much goes into making something short, huh?

Let's keep going. What happens after she's said yes and he gets in the car (or the buggy, if you are writing historical) and they drive away?

This is your wrap-up. The final moment where we have that proof this couple wasn't just in lust, but love. There's a promise made, a vow. "I'll love you forever." This is where they talk about the future, how they'll always be together. It's what makes the reader smile, warms their heart, and cements their belief that an instant connection can be real.

Because isn't that our goal? To make the reader sigh with content, close the pages...and then go see what else you've written to give them that feeling again and again and again?

Okay. Are you ready to move on and learn some more about writing your story, but also polishing it? Let's go on to the final part of this book. You're going to learn what you need to do to send this story out into the world.

PART 4: SENDING YOUR BOOK INTO THE WORLD

The First Draft Is Not a Final Draft

For many, the chapter title comes as a surprise. However, this is an important thing to remember. Your first completed draft should not be the one your readers who have bought your book should see. *My* first drafts aren't ones I want my readers to see! There's usually something wrong story or character wise that just isn't working, and the typos? Since I could spend forever editing my own book, making teeny tweaks and never progressing, I have to make myself just write and take care of that at the end, so I actually finish.

It's been my experience as a reader first, then an editor, and finally an author, that far too many people write their books, upload right away, and then wonder why their book doesn't do well. Matter of fact, I saw that today in an author group on Facebook. The author was angry they'd been left a one-star review, and talked about how they were still tweaking the manuscript because they'd only just finished it. That's a big no! Never upload, and then tweak. Get your story the best it can be before you upload.

You know that saying, there's only one chance to make a first impression? It's true! Once you have a reputation as an author who _________ (insert blank there) it can be tricky to change opinions. It's important to give readers books the way you want to be recognized from the start.

Think about it. What makes you put down a book? I've read my share of books that were so poorly written, it didn't matter that the cover was stunning and the blurb interesting. The typos, poor punctuation, grammar, and plot holes were difficult to see past. It was either returned or I did not finish.

You don't want that, my friend. You do not want to be someone's DNF. You also don't want to have a poor review left. Nothing makes me sadder than seeing someone with a low review for something like typos, poor punctuation, grammar, and plot holes. They happen. Oh yes, they do. But that's why you don't make your first draft your final version. Get your mistakes corrected as much as humanly possible before they are mentioned in a review.

Of course, there is always the danger that if you send out advance copies before a final proofread, someone will mention things in a review that they found and you corrected in your final version. It's happened to me. It's the first review listed, too, sadly. The person got an advance reader copy. I was clear that it had not had the second proofread that I give myself when I sent it, and I was currently working on that. They still left a review saying there were some typos. My heart sank. So much so, the fact the others were glowing and the person had mentioned they'd read it twice now and still liked it dulled some of my joy, when ordinarily, I'd have been thrilled someone read it twice and loved it. I don't want that for you!

What happened afterward? Well, I learned my lesson. I never again sent out an ARC without it being proofread by my proofreader, and then again by me. It's a strict rule I have for myself. That's why I want my lesson to be one you get to live vicariously through! Not in actuality. Reviews linger, even if we don't want them to.

When it comes to getting your book ready for readers, it needs to be the best that it can be. That means that you need to go over it a few times before you send it off into the world of beta readers or editors. And, before you dismiss the idea of them because you don't think your budget can handle it, please let me explain the importance of each in the next chapter. As an aside, I can promise you that the better condition your story is in, the less it will cost you for an edit. If your editor can focus purely on your story because you've done the things like spellcheck and read it a few times and tried to make it the best you can, you will also get it back faster!

Now, I get it. You are writing short romance. You might be aiming for one a week, so you don't want to take too much time poring over your story. You don't want three or four drafts, plus your editing or proofread. I understand totally.

But.

You just can't send that first draft out into the world yet. You need to go over it, at least once, but preferably more than that, and make sure it's the best that it can be before it moves on to your support team, like beta readers, editors, proofreaders, or readers.

It's a strange phenomenon how when we are reading the things that we write, our mind fills in the little gaps there. We have missing words, but our brain knows what should be there, so puts it in for us, and our eyes think they've read them, when a fresh set of eyes (reader, editor, etc.) would be like, yikes! Something is missing! The same goes for typos. It's even worse when you are tired, on too tight of a deadline, or distracted.

Please. Don't do that to yourself. Give your readers the stories they crave, and the excellence you are capable of! They, and you, deserve to have it as good as you can get it.

Notice, I didn't say perfect. There's no such thing as a perfect book. But you can get it pretty darn close. Readers read because they want to be entertained. They want to enjoy the story. An extra comma? Won't throw them off. However, having too many typos or missing words is going to make the readers notice. That's why another pair of eyes and a second read-through on your part is critical.

I understand that not everyone wants to use an editor. However, if you choose not to get outside help, at least make your book the best you can before you upload it, by self-editing. That means going through and reading it top to bottom carefully, correcting all the mistakes that you can. Sometimes, you'll need to do that several times because each time you might see something you missed previously.

There are a few tricks you can use to help you spot mistakes that you missed while reading in your Word doc.

Use the Read Aloud Feature

This is a favorite feature of a friend. Even after she uses an editor, she will ask Word to read it to her. Sometimes, she finds mistakes that were missed.

Read it Out Loud to Yourself

Reading your book out loud will help prevent your eyes from skipping over mistakes that your brain thinks aren't there, simply because you are engaging another sense.

Print Your Manuscript

It's amazing how different a story looks on paper. Sometimes, typos leap out at you. I'd suggest also printing it in a slightly larger and a very neutral font, so that you can read it more easily. Sometimes, specialty fonts or those that are too narrow can make one letter look like an entirely different one.

Step Away

Would you like to know the absolute simplest way to get your story the best it can be before you email it to your support team? Here it is.

Put it away for a week or two, at the minimum.

Yep. Move on to your next project, let some time pass, and then reread your story. You might find that it's just as you'd hoped—and maybe even brings you to swoony tears. But what you also might find is that you've got some typos. That Elaine's name, halfway through, switched to Ellen. (Ask me how I know! See? First drafts aren't the final draft!) You might even see that the logistics of how you'd had something just aren't possible timeline wise.

That's why the time you spend looking over what you've written, when you've set it aside for a little and can see it with fresh eyes, is incredibly valuable. After your second reading and making tweaks, you have a better, stronger book.

To learn about the different types of professional editing, and what a beta reader can and can't do, head to the next chapter.

Editing

Before we dive into types of editing, I want to share why I became an editor—and why finding the right editor matters so much.

Decades ago, I had a soul-crushing experience with an editor. This was back before digital submissions. You'd print your manuscript, send it over, and get back red ink and possibly coffee stains. I got a little more than that too. I'd approached her because I'd come close, so, so close with a few agents and a small press, but my book was still passed over. I wondered why, and asked her to help me improve the story.

Not only did this editor shred my middle grade fantasy manuscript, but she was pretty awful about it. Her comments in the margins like "are you kidding me?" and "that's stupid" and "you should do this" and "this is boring" killed my love of writing. After all, if an editor had said such a thing it must be true, yes? It was many, many years before I opened the desk drawer I'd shoved it into and looked at it again, wondering if I was still a horrible writer.

And do you know what? As I read through those first pages, going over her comments and my words, I saw something that made me confused. Things she'd left big angry red pen marks on weren't errors. They weren't plot holes. They were things she didn't like because she personally didn't like those things. Many of the corrections she'd made were style choices, and not necessary. They were something done just to look like something had been done.

I felt sick to my stomach, but I thought the only way I'd ever know if my instincts were right was to get another set of eyes on it. So, I sent it to another editor, one I'd seen others recommending.

Now, at this point, we'd moved into the digital age, where it was done through emails, not paper copies. When I got the book back, I couldn't believe my eyes. She enhanced my words. Made my work shine. I was in love with it again. My story was there, not turned into something I didn't write. Her helpful comments made in comment boxes explained why she suggested something. She didn't just tell me to do it, because she knew everything there was to know about editing and I was just an author. She taught me what I needed.

And once my heart had stopped pounding in fear over what I had worried I'd see—a second person telling me I was a horrible writer—I knew that I had discovered what I wanted to do. Support authors. Help make their work shine and encourage them. That's why I've spent as much time as I have editing for others, giving classes on the craft of writing, keeping up to date with editing trends, and also writing this book. I want to help everyone I come across have the feeling of being proud about what they wrote.

It's my firm belief that there is no book, not a one, that can't be fixed with a little work and some clever tweaks.

If right now you are reading this and thinking, "Well, that's a great story, but it's still not in my budget. I hear good stuff about getting free beta readers," I get that. But will you at least read this chapter? You're already here. Let me just explain what editors do, and even touch on beta readers. Then you can figure out what's best for you at this stage in your career.

The Elephant in the Room

Let me take a second to address AI editing. It is something many authors want to do because then they can do everything themselves. Sounds good, right?

AI tools like Grammarly and ProWritingAid can catch basic errors, but they can't evaluate story logic, character consistency, or whether your romance is emotionally satisfying. They also don't take into consideration context and can even introduce errors into your manuscript. It's okay to use them, but use them as a first pass, not a replacement for human editing. They are assistive tools, meaning they are there to assist the human. Not replace them.

Some authors also choose to use generative AI, such as ChatGPT or Gemini. This form of AI has much more control over the manuscript, and will often completely rewrite it. I still feel strongly against those. If you really want to use it for brainstorming, sure. But for writing? Or asking it to make your writing better? It doesn't always. After a while, readers, not just editors, can tell that you used AI. And, for the author who doesn't remember to remove those prompts or look things over to make sure their characters would really talk that way and that no inconsistencies or repetitions were introduced? It can come back to haunt them.

Remember, you want to start off on the right foot with your readers by giving them your best.

Choosing an Editor

If you are new to the world of having your book edited, it might surprise you to learn that there are several types of editors. Some editors are trained in developmental, copy or line edits, and proofreads. Others specialize only in one of those areas. And, to further add to the conversation, there are some editors who only work on specific genres.

Editors come in all price ranges as well, and you can find them and their rates quite easily online. You can browse a place such as the Editorial Freelancers Association (EFA) for a list of its members and suggested rates, and you can also go to sites that connect authors with editors, such as Upwork. I personally use Upwork to fill in gaps in my schedule, and find it's not overly complicated to use. Many people like it because it lets them browse a huge list of editors and see their reviews.

If word of mouth is your preferred way of seeking help, ask around and see who uses whom for their editing. Asking in a Facebook group or even by email is sure to get you a few names.

But, what happens after you've reached out to an editor? That's what I'm here to share with you.

There are some incredibly important things to keep in mind when it comes to working with an editor. Here is what I think you should be aware of, from my perspective as an author and an editor.

Editors do not all charge the same rate

While on the surface, it makes sense that not all editors charge the same, something that you need to be aware of is that the different types of editing also have different rates. While it will vary between individual editors, you can expect to pay more for a developmental edit than you would for a proofread.

Why? Because of the time spent. I'm going to break down each of the types of editing for you shortly, so you can see just what goes into each.

> **Just because an editor charges less doesn't make them a bad editor**

I feel like I have to put this one out there, even though (and especially among editors) those who charge less than industry rates can get looked down on. The fact of the matter is that while editors would love to charge industry rates, there are many, many talented authors, such as yourself, who are on a budget. And so many of us editors get that.

However, the best way to know if an editor is actually a good one, and not just going to pretend all is well after running your manuscript through AI or a spellchecker, is to ask for testimonials, and ask for a free sample edit.

While some may suggest asking an editor for a portfolio or a list of authors they've edited for, the truth is that while sometimes we can tell you, far too many times we are tied up by an NDA. Truthfully, I've lost out on some jobs I'd have loved to have had because I couldn't share that I'd done similar work, since it was for a celebrity or a professional athlete's child. I had signed ironclad NDAs.

If an editor tells you she can't share a portfolio or a list of authors they've worked with, that's not a deal breaker. Truthfully, it might not even help you at all, even if you got those lists. Why? Because your manuscript is its own unique story. When I'm asked to share an editing sample from a previous client, I'm quick to explain that the edits I made for one person may not be the right kinds of edits for another.

So, instead of asking for a client list, ask for:

- A sample edit of your work

- General testimonials (many editors have these on their websites)

- Their experience in your specific genre

Sometimes, you can even see those things on third-party platforms, and get yourself familiar with the editor before you even reach out. For example, on Upwork, you can see how many jobs they've done, the ratings others have given them, sometimes even a portfolio or a video, and feel a bit better about what you'll get if you work with that person.

Never feel bad either about asking if you can jump on a call or a Zoom with someone, just to get a feel for them. An honest editor won't have an issue with that. And, even if you don't go with them, they know it's part of the job. The same with if we do a sample edit, and you choose to go elsewhere. So, let's mention that.

You can ask for a sample edit

If one isn't offered, it's okay to ask for a sample edit. Most editors will copy or line edit 1,000–1,500 words for free. This sample edit will give an example of what your actual edit will look like. It isn't really possible to developmentally edit a sample, as the section would be too small. A reasonable request would be to ask if you could pay for them to developmentally edit a chapter or two, to see what kind of feedback you get.

Ask for a contract

The majority of editors have contracts. They protect you, they protect them. Third-party platforms that connect authors with editors have a built-in contract. However, if you want an NDA, you'll need to provide that and request they sign it if it's not already built into an editor's contract. Contracts when working directly with an editor are usually digital signatures. Many editors don't worry about contracts for repeat clients, or they use an email to serve as their contract, if they feel comfortable.

Payment terms

Payment terms vary by editor. Some request half to start, some payment in full. This is where a contract is helpful. Some third-party sites (like Upwork) hold your funds in escrow, meaning they aren't released until the work is complete. When working with an editor directly, you can expect to be invoiced through a third-party site like Wave or PayPal or Venmo. It's important to find out what the payment terms will be. If you've questions, for example, or need a payment plan (which is most common with manuscripts more than 100k in size) be sure to be clear and upfront with that, to see if it's offered.

Don't be afraid to ask questions

It is so important to ask your questions. I can assure you, editors don't mind one bit. Typically, when I'm approached, I'll answer their questions in the initial email, but as I send over my sample edit, I explain what I did and what working with me might look like, should they think we are a good fit. I go over things like how I communicate during an edit, my general timeline, how I invoice, the rate they will pay, and how they are welcome to ask me any questions at all, at any point.

I try to be thorough, because I know that passing off your work to an editor can be a scary and overwhelming thing. Don't be embarrassed to ask how something works. We want to help you.

> **Sending over a manuscript the best it can be will cost you less**

I mentioned this earlier, but it's so, so true. My friend, if you send me a manuscript over that's little more than a first draft, with no quotation marks around the dialogue and All The Words Capitalized Because It Looks Cool, and more plot holes than that baby Swiss cheese in my fridge, then it's going to take me far longer to get your story reader-ready, and you are going to still have to weigh in on those story issues and give your manuscript a little more TLC.

However, if you send me over something where I can see at a glance you did the best you could, I'm going to have it back to you faster, and at a lower rate. Even if an editor charges a flat rate per hour or per word, that's still going to be based on the time they feel it needs. When an editor knows that manuscript A needs more work than manuscript B, the per-word rate may increase and that's why you often get a range when asking for an estimate before they've seen your work.

> **Beta readers are not editors**

Beta readers who you get for free are wonderful, but they serve a different purpose than editors or those who offer professional beta reading services that are paid. A beta reader gives you reader feedback on plot and characters. Editors give you professional craft feedback and polish. Ideally, you want both.

And, just like with anyone else, you'll have some who are better than others. A common complaint by authors is their beta readers tell them everything's great, when they knew it wasn't, and wanted an outside perspective on where their plot was sagging or why the story just felt blah. On that same note, some authors also get upset when their beta readers aren't finding typos and errors. That's not their job. Their main job is to read and tell you what they thought of your book as a reader.

Beta readers are fantastic and helpful, but they are also (likely) busy humans who are reading just to read first, and be helpful second. They also don't have the same kind of training that a professional editor does. They might mistakenly think that you don't need to hyphenate a word or that there's a comma needed here and not there. If they do something more, like catch some typos, fantastic. But you shouldn't expect them to do the job of an editor, not when they aren't being paid and likely don't have that skill set.

The different types of editors

As I'd mentioned, there are different types of editors. If this is your first book or you're struggling with plot, you'll want to seek out a developmental edit. If your story works but needs polishing, look for a copy or line edit. If you've already edited thoroughly, what you are looking for is a proofread. If your budget is tight, look for a hybrid edit or, at minimum, a proofread.

If that all sounded a little confusing, don't worry! I'm going to explain a little about each of those types of editors right now.

Developmental Editors

Developmental editing focuses on the big picture elements of a manuscript, evaluating its core concepts, structure, plot, characters, and overall effectiveness to ensure it is a compelling story that meets the author's goals and resonates with the target audience. This type of editing addresses macro-level issues like the narrative arc, pacing, worldbuilding, and theme, rather than grammar or typos, which are handled in later editing stages.

A developmental edit, should you choose to do one, comes before any other type of editing. The reason for that is if there is to be a large story change, you don't want to pay twice for copy edits or proofreading.

The feedback given in your developmental edit might be done in-line in your manuscript, using comment boxes to call out particular areas, but it is typically given to you in an editorial report, the length of which varies. This report will go over everything from concerns with the plot or characters, to the structure, theme, and worldbuilding. You'll get a detailed analysis of your manuscript, its strengths and weaknesses, and also constructive feedback with suggestions and guidance for improving it.

Line and Copy Editors

While used interchangeably at times, there is a distinct difference between the two. A line edit is much heavier. It's striking out sentences or moving paragraphs around, more so than correcting a few words here and there. Regardless, both are the same in that they go through, top to bottom, word by word in your manuscript.

The following is the list of things that I check for when I'm doing a line edit or copyedit.

- Every word checked carefully for clarity and flow

- Spelling, grammar, syntax, punctuation, and capitalization checks

- Removal of redundant words that slow the story

- Consistency in tenses

- Replacement of awkward passages

- Proper spacing for words, lines, and paragraphs

- Effectiveness of sentence structure and word choice

- Seamless transitions

- Enough detail

- Characters

- Anything that can improve your story while maintaining your style and tone

The things an editor might offer with your manuscript may be different, but that's a general guideline of what they might be working on, when editing your manuscript.

Hybrid Editing

If you are in need of a combination of developmental edits and copy edits, but you don't have the budget for both separately, ask your editor if they can do them at the same time, in one round. Hybrid editing combines developmental and copy editing in one pass, making it more affordable while still addressing both story-level and sentence-level issues. Many editors offer this as a standard service. Essentially, what happens is that your editor will go through, correcting errors as they see them, making adjustments to your text, but also pointing out those plot issues in a comment box, leaving them for you to fix on your own.

When I line or copy edit, I offer this automatically, asked or not. If I see something, I'm never going to ignore it. That would make us both look bad! However, there are some editors who don't do it, or if they do, know it by another name or no name at all, so ask if it's something you want, just to ensure you get it.

Proofreaders

This is the final step. Proofreading is there to catch any final typos or punctuation errors before publication. It is especially helpful if you added more after editing. From my website, this is what I personally look at while proofreading.

- Full word by word check

- Consistency in text and story

- Punctuation

- Spelling

- Homophones

- Paragraphs and line breaks

- Consistent spelling and grammar

- Extra letter and line spaces

- Anything else that might have been missed by editing

Fees

As a very general guide, since rates vary, you might see proofreading rates from $0.0025–0.015+ per word, copy editing $0.005–0.02+ per word, and developmental editing $0.01–0.03+ per word. This means a 20,000-word novella might cost anywhere from $50–$600 or more depending on the service. Always request a quote for your project.

As you can see, there's a bit more to editing than simply finding misspelled words and wrangling errant punctuation marks. An editor is an incredibly important member of your publishing team. However, let me end this chapter with a warning.

Your editor needs some advance notice. Some book quite far in advance; others do multiple projects at once. It takes far longer to edit a book than to simply read it, as your editor is reading very, very slowly, and checking each word, confirming the spelling of countries, towns, etc., being sure each punctuation mark is appropriate, and often scrolling back to previous parts of the book to check something.

While each editor works at a different speed, you can expect, on average, your editor to request two to three weeks working time on a novella of 20,000, longer for more extensive edits or during busy seasons. Rush fees may apply for faster turnaround. Get your return date from them, but be very wary of anyone who says they can get your 40k back to you in a day or two. It might not be a quality human edit.

FORMATTING

It's not enough to write *The End* and then get your book edited. Formatting is critical, especially if you want to look professional and also meet the technical specifications of the place you are uploading, so that your book can be processed, printed, and displayed.

Proper formatting is also what makes your manuscript look like a polished book, and not just a Word document. You've worked so hard creating your story! Don't skimp. Poor formatting makes you and your book look bad.

Before you go to format, there's something you need to make sure your book has. That's your front matter and your back matter sandwiching the body of your book. While some things are standard, such as the copyright page and table of contents, other things are optional, such as listing additional titles.

Here's a suggestion of what is usually in the front and back matter.

Front matter:

- Title Page

- Copyright

- Dedication

- Table of Contents

Back matter:

- Author Bio

- Info on where readers can find you

- List of other books you've written

- Newsletter signup/reader magnet

- Sneak peek of another book

Each front matter item typically gets its own page, while back matter can be more flexible in layout. When it comes to the body of your manuscript (the chapters) while it's author style choice, the majority of authors choose to start chapters on the right side of their book.

A quick note on an ISBN or an ASIN. When you self-publish, the platform you use will usually give you a free ISBN or ASIN (Amazon Standard Identification Number). You get one for each publishing format. However, it is for use only on that platform.

If you want to buy your own ISBN, you can. In the US, you need to buy ISBNs from Bowker. They are the only ones who sell them. The more you buy, a package of ten versus one, the cheaper it is. In some other countries, there is no charge for them. The choice is yours. I do not buy an ISBN for my eBooks, but I do for my paperbacks.

Now, ready to talk about how you do this formatting thing I've been going on about? There are multiple ways. Some people do the formatting on their own through Microsoft Word. Others use a free service or a paid program. I'll share some of those shortly. I'm not recommending one way over another, so I'd suggest asking around. It will vary, too, between Apple and PC as to which paid program you can use.

The main things to look for are:

- **Readability:** The correct use of font size, font type, line spacing, and paragraph indentation makes the book comfortable and easy to read.

- **Consistency:** Formatting creates a uniform look throughout the entire book—all of your chapter titles look the same, all of the body text is styled the same, and all headers/footers (if used) are consistent.

- **Navigation:** Proper formatting is what generates the clickable Table of Contents that readers can use to go between chapters in an eBook.

For eBooks, formatting ensures your digital file (like an ePub or a Word doc) can be converted into a reflowable format that works on all Kindle devices and apps. A reflowable format refers to the text and other elements being flexible and able to adjust automatically to fit the screen size, orientation, and personal preferences of the reader.

And, because nothing in life is simple, it's going to be a tad different when formatting an eBook versus a paperback.

For print books, printers need a perfectly setup PDF file to print your book correctly. Formatting your paperback deals with:

- **Trim Size:** This sets the dimensions of the finished book, like 5x8, etc.

- **Margins:** This is where text is placed so it doesn't get cut off on the edges or in the gutter during the printing and trimming process.

- **Bleed:** If you have images or color that go to the edge of the page, formatting makes sure they extend past the trim line so no white space appears after the book is cut.

With a paperback, you'll need your book description (blurb) ready for the back cover, so prepare that before ordering your cover wrap (the full paperback cover including front, spine, and back).

If you don't format yourself, be sure to be specific with your formatter and tell them just what you are wanting, and the final format or size of the book if it's a paperback, along with the page count that you are needing and if you are printing on white or cream paper so you get just what you are hoping for.

While some people enjoy formatting their books, others outsource to someone else. Here are just a few of the ways books can be formatted:

- Through a Word doc

- With a third-party software such as Vellum (popular but for Mac only), Atticus (cross-platform), or Draft2Digital (free formatting service).

- Hiring a formatter on Fiverr/Upwork/through word of mouth.

There's no wrong way; it's whatever works for you. It's just important to be sure you do format. That's what gets it to a professional-looking book that meets the industry standards and the publishing requirements of whatever platform you're using.

BOOK COVERS

This might be one of the most fun parts of publishing because it means you are nearly at the finish line. When it comes to choosing a book cover, there's a bit more to it than just finding a picture that you like online, slapping it into Canva, and uploading. You know how they say don't judge a book by its cover?

Well, be honest. We all do. And so do your readers. You'll want an on-brand cover for your book, and unless you've had a ton of experience, you might not want to be DIYing your first few covers. What we might think looks good might not actually be. One of the best ways you can tell if you are on point with your cover is to browse the Top 100 in your category in the Kindle store.

Could the cover you made blend right in? If so, awesome! You've got a talent I sure lack. If it's pretty different, sometimes different isn't good. Book covers are one of those things. You might want to consider hiring someone, and getting someone who is familiar with your genre cover needs.

I'm going to be quite up front with you. I've dozens of books, and I don't make covers. All those details? That patience required? The knowing which fonts work and how to do layers so things look amazing and not homemade?

This girl does not have the patience or skill for that.

If you are feeling the same, or even if you are just curious about why getting a cover designer might be a good idea, let me walk you through what to do when seeking out your cover designer.

Finding a Cover Designer

Just like with getting a sample edit done, ask to browse covers. The nice thing about working with a cover artist is they come in all price ranges and will be able to show you the covers they made. Very few cover designers need to sign an NDA. Most actually have it in contracts that they are to be listed on the copyright page and allowed to use the images in their portfolios.

Where can you find a cover designer? Again, like with editing, you can seek third-party sites, such as Upwork or Fiverr and word of mouth. I've gotten lovely covers off of Fiverr (read reviews!) and an author acquaintance has a woman she adores on Etsy. The majority of my covers come from a cover designer in my author circle who makes them, knows how to keep me on brand with my genre, and isn't scared to tell me when something I want isn't going to work. The best part is, we've worked together on so many covers, that sometimes I can tell her I have an idea for a book, and before I finish telling her what I think I might do, she's dropped a cover draft in the chat and it's perfect.

Understanding Cover Licensing

There's a whole issue with copyrights and licensing, and proper licensing of images. Did you know that if you went to get a stock photo, it might be good for only so many copies? And it also might only be for digital? Or just print? Or, not even allowed to be used at all, because it's just for editorial? Or there's a copyright on it, and it's not really a stock image at all?

It's true! While you might really love an image you've found on the internet, that doesn't mean it's something you are allowed to use. Even on Canva. That's why working with a cover designer who knows what they are doing is important! They'll help keep you safe with legalities.

Stock photos come with licenses that specify:

- How many copies you can sell (extended licenses may remove this limit)

- Whether it can be used for print, digital, or both

- Whether you have exclusive rights

A good cover designer handles all licensing properly and builds those costs into their quote.

What Your Cover Designer Needs

When the time comes for you to get your book cover, you need to decide what ways you are going to publish. Are you going to just do an eBook? Do you want to do a paperback as well? What about a large print or an audiobook? You'll need a different cover for each way you publish, so it's important to know what you want so you can communicate that with your cover designer.

Prices for book covers range from double digits to four digits. Be sure to ask questions and see what's included. Your eBook cover isn't the same thing as a paperback cover, and in order to get your paperback wrap, you'll need to have your book formatted, so you can share specific details with your cover creator, such as the size, the page type, and the page count. This information comes from your formatted manuscript and your chosen print platform. These details will affect the cover file size, and your cover designer will need to know your:

- Trim size (5x8, 6x9, etc.)

- Page count (this affects spine width)

- Paper type (cream vs. white affects thickness)

- Bleed requirements

You'll also want to be sure you have your book description at the ready, so they can put that on there for you.

Custom Versus Premade Covers

Depending on your budget, you might choose a custom-made cover, where you specify the details you want, including color choices for clothing. Or, you might be browsing premade covers, ones the cover designer has made already, and think that it's perfect. Sometimes, they are willing to make more covers in that style, so that you can buy them for a series. Not sure of the difference?

- **Premade covers** are less expensive ($50–$150 as a

ballpark), offer you faster turnaround, but usually have limited customizations available.

- **Custom covers** are more expensive ($200–$500+ as a ballpark), are fully personalized, and have a longer timeline to receive.

Some designers now offer AI-generated covers at lower price points. Be aware that some readers and reviewers strongly oppose AI art. Also be aware that if you use AI art, you don't own a copyright on it. If there are AI elements in the cover or it is an AI cover in its entirety, your designer should disclose this so you can make an informed choice, and can check any boxes on the platform that you upload on stating the cover has AI within it so that you are fully transparent and don't get in trouble with that distributor.

Working with Your Designer

When it comes to working with your cover designer, be prepared with just a little more than your trim size, page count, page color, and bleed information. To improve the chances of getting the cover you envision on the first try:

- Provide comp titles (books with covers you like)

- Share your blurb so they understand the mood

- Be specific about what you don't want

- Expect a few rounds of revisions (see how many are included in your price)

In case it was a concern you've had, there's very little need to worry about your cover being sold to someone else. The cover designer who made your cover won't let anyone else have it. Is it possible that there might be something similar? Yes, but it shouldn't ever be exact. Go look at mountain man or billionaire or mail-order bride or cowboy covers. Similar in feel, but not too similar in covers, unless it's a series. That's just those other covers matching their genre.

While it's true that some popular stock models pop up often (especially in historical, where we have fewer to choose from) that's when finding a cover artist to change the color of a dress or do a head swap on a model is an asset, as is seeking out lesser known models from stock footage sites.

Cover Design Best Practices

What else do you need to think about when it comes to book covers?

- Text needs to be readable when it's small

- Simple but bold designs work better than intricate ones

- Test your cover at thumbnail size before approving

Genre Expectations: Staying On Brand

That all said, there's something you need to know about book covers, and you might not like hearing. The book cover is not *for you* to admire and love. It's for *the reader*. And, just like in a Regency novel, there are expectations put upon people. You, my friend, are expected to be on brand, within genre expectations. That means if you are writing a bite-sized romcom, the cover had best not be a stock photo of a beach with sandals on the cover. If you are writing a western, you cannot choose a city with a skyline and the sunset peeking behind it. If you are writing a historical set in the 1800s, you absolutely cannot be using a modern day looking model on the front.

What should you look for? Romcoms need bright colors, fun fonts, and often illustrated or cartoony styles. Westerns need cowboys, horses, and ranches. Regency needs period-appropriate clothing and settings like gardens or manor homes. Browse the top sellers in your genre to see what others are doing. Take notes of the style, the colors, the feel. Can you tell just at a glance what kind of book it's going to be from the cover? That's just what you want to do also. Your cover should fit on that virtual bookshelf, right alongside those other bestsellers.

"But a different style cover stands out, I've been told." Sure does. And tells your reader who loves their western books with a man in a cowboy hat that your cover with a girl in a coffee shop isn't for her.

That first impression is everything. We judge books by their covers, remember? I've got covers I really didn't care for. Some I had control over, some I didn't. But, I'll be darned if one of them that I just can't stand, and is similar to the others in that multi-author series, gets so many compliments. I was a newer author at the time, and trusted my cover designer. It paid off.

Personal preferences sometimes have to be set aside. That's not to say you'll end up with covers you don't like. It's also not to say that there won't be times you can't have something you want, so that your book blends in with the others in your subgenre, and you stand a better chance of attracting readers.

Cover designers create, day in and day out. People return to them, and they are, just like editors, always keeping an eye on publishing trends and all of the other things they need to do to stay current with covers and help their authors be on point with their genre's cover expectations.

Timeline and Final Tips

Just like when choosing an editor, don't be afraid to ask your future or current cover designer questions about the process, and what you can do to ensure you are happy with your cover.

A final word of warning, though. Just like with an editor, you cannot assume that they can get your cover to you within a few days. Some cover designers can; others are booked months in advance. Don't wait until the last minute.

Ready to start learning a little about marketing? Let's head to the next chapter.

CHOOSING YOUR PRICE POINT

I'd be remiss if I didn't mention the price that you might sell your short romance at. Since I only sell my eBooks on Amazon, I can't speak to how it works beyond KDP.

If you were to jump on Amazon right now, you'd likely see prices anywhere from .99 to even $5.99 for a story. The majority are set at .99 and $2.99. But before you settle on a price for your books, there's something you need to think about.

The price you sell your book at is not your royalty rate. Any eBook listed for sale on Amazon under $2.99 will only receive a 35% royalty. An eBook that is $2.99 or more will receive a 70% royalty. This is going to vary by a few pennies for the delivery charge we authors pay for the book to be transferred, but generally, the royalty on a .99 eBook is around thirty-five cents, and the royalty on an eBook listed at $2.99 is $2.09.

Great! So that means all your books should be listed at $2.99 for maximum royalties? Not necessarily. Let's go over a few pros and cons in pricing.

Pricing Lower

Think about what you'd pay. Remember we talked about the short categories? Books that fall into a fifteen or thirty minute read? Would you want to pay $2.99 for fifteen minutes or less of a story?

While it's tempting to say, "Well, if my expenses were $100 to create this short story, the higher I sell it at, the faster I make my money back and also make a profit," it's important to take into consideration your current reader level. If you are a new author, having your book listed at .99, especially if it's a bite-sized read, might make someone willing to take a chance on a new-to-them author. That's also why many authors will have their books in Kindle Unlimited. Readers are much more likely to try a new author without a big financial commitment.

Pricing Higher

If you have a book that's 15,000 words or more, then I think you ought to have it for $2.99. After all, you spent a long time creating that book. You can still put it on sale, but you are teaching readers that though you charge $2.99 for a book, it's going to be worth every penny.

There is something to be said about the perceived value. If we get something for free or .99, we might not value it the same as we would if we paid more. Do you ever hit thrift stores or yard sales for paperbacks? Do those get read as quickly as the ones you paid full price for? Quite possibly not.

Middle of the Road Strategy

Now, none of what I've said means you can't put your book on sale or even for free. If you are enrolled in KDP select it's very easy to do both. It's scheduled, and Amazon does all the work for you. If you are writing in a series, many authors will do the first book in the series for .99 to hook readers. That's a great happy medium. So is taking several of your bite-sized romances and box-setting them into a collection for a low price.

Say, you'd usually charge $2.99 each. Why not take five of those, put them in a set, and charge $9.99? Your readers feel like they got a deal, and you've got new readers. Some only like to read box sets. It also looks like one heck of a deal when that box set goes for half off, and they've got the deal of a dollar a book.

The same could be done with a bunch of .99 eBooks. Bundle them, discount slightly, and occasionally put them on sale.

A Final Word

A final thought on pricing your books. Do you remember in the chapter before this one, I explained how you need to have similar covers to your subgenre? The same goes for pricing. If all of your peers are releasing at $2.99, and you are releasing at .99, readers may have that perceived idea that your book isn't as good.

By that same logic, if they are all releasing at .99, and you price at $2.99, readers might think you are too expensive, and not be interested in reading your book.

Just like with getting cover ideas, see what others in your subgenre are doing. You want to blend in, be right there with them, not so drastically different your book stands out in a bad way.

KEYWORDS AND CATEGORIES

While this is just a short chapter, it's also an important one. The last time you wanted to find something online, but didn't know the exact words, what did you do?

Let me share what I did earlier today. I searched for:

Anime with kid who saves the world appropriate for twelve-year-old.

And do you know what? Lots popped up! Google is amazing. We've come so far since the early days. Now, anything you want you can find. And...suggestions for other things pop up. That's where this gets really interesting.

"Great," I hear you saying. "I already know all about Google. But what about Amazon? How is that going to help me?" Simple. It's the same principle! A search pulls up items, and clicking lets the reader find books to their taste, and hopefully yours.

So, let's go briefly into how keywords and categories can help point readers to just what they want—your books.

Keywords

I was trying to explain how keywords work to a friend, so do this little exercise with me. What's something you love to read? Protector romance? Mail-order bride book? Marriage of convenience story?

Go pop that into the Amazon search bar. I'll wait.

Hey! You're back. Did you do it? If yes, fantastic. Find anything good? If not...well, you missed the important part of the lesson. But it's all good. I'm not going to keep it a secret.

Keywords are the thing that is going to make your book findable. When you go to set up your book in the KDP dashboard, they ask for your keywords. They tell you that you can have up to seven, because there are seven fields to enter your stuff in.

Does that mean you only get seven single words?

Nope!

Fill those babies.

Of course, you have to use the space wisely. There's only so much room, right? And you don't want to use keywords that aren't going to help people find your book. You want to use ones that are relevant to your book.

Here's an example from one of mine, since I write historical romance:

Sweet and clean historical western romance

1800s pioneer and frontier romance west

He falls first historical romance clean

Inspirational romance runaway bride

Grumpy sunshine short story Oregon Trail

I don't want to bore you with all seven lines, but you see what I'm doing there? I'm putting in keywords, things that are in my book. See what else is there? Sing it with me!

Tropes!

I've got some he falls first and grumpy sunshine and runaway bride going on. I've also got the things that will point readers looking for clean or inspirational romance toward my books.

When it comes time to choose your keywords, think about what readers might search for:

- Tropes (fake dating, enemies to lovers, second chance)

- Setting (small town, cowboy, Regency)

- Subgenre descriptors (clean romance, sweet romance, inspirational)

- Mood/tone (heartwarming, funny, emotional)

Each of those seven fields can hold (at the time of writing this) up to fifty characters including spaces, so you can pack in multiple related terms per line. That's why I can fit "Sweet and clean historical western romance" in one field.

You can also look for keyword suggestions by seeing what other authors put into their blurbs, using a paid program like Publisher Rocket, checking the K-lytics reports that can be bought, or seeing what the different categories are that other authors are using, and use some of those keywords.

However, there are some important things NOT to do when it comes to choosing keywords:

- Don't use competitor author names (against Amazon's Terms of Service)

- Don't use trademarked terms you don't own

- Don't keyword stuff with irrelevant popular terms just for visibility

Something you might not realize is you can change your keywords anytime. If your book isn't getting found, or you realized you've got a trope in there you didn't mention but is pretty popular, go in and change it!

Categories

There's another way for readers to find your book, and that's by putting it into the category they might browse. Amazon does an incredible job of breaking down categories. I'm going to use western, for example. Not only is there a western category under romance, but also under inspirational, under Christian, and under genre fiction. I've not even looked to see the YA or teen categories because I don't write for those ages, but I bet they have it too.

My point is, you'll want to choose what's best for your particular book. Categories are organized in hierarchies. For example: Romance > Historical > Western & Frontier (where I have many of my books) means I click Romance, then Historical, then Western & Frontier. There are many subcategories within the larger categories, and there will be something that fits your story well. Sometimes, the tough part is just choosing three.

The more specific you get when selecting your categories, the easier it is to rank as a bestseller in that smaller category. Be sure to look over your options before you decide. I choose the three categories we are allowed to have based on my book. If I have a Christmas title, I'm going to choose at least one holiday category. Then, I have placement a little wider than just in one spot.

Just like keywords, your categories can be updated and changed at any time. Some authors like to be in smaller categories in order to improve their chances of a new release banner.

But...here's the thing that no one usually tells you. It comes in the form of looking at your listing. Your jaw may drop, you might gasp, "But that's not the category I chose!" And that reaction and gasp might be a good one, or it might be bad. The reason for that is even though we choose our categories, Amazon can decide if they want to keep us there.

Sometimes, you get moved to something they feel fits better. Sometimes it does...and sometimes it doesn't. The more accurate you are in choosing your categories, the better the chance of being where you want to be.

There is an interesting thing, though, about when Amazon puts you into a category you didn't choose. While I won't call them secret categories, because you can see when your book is put into them, Amazon does have categories that you cannot choose yourself.

Do you remember in Chapter 1 I talked about the short-read categories?

- 15 minutes
- 30 minutes

- 45 minutes

- 1 hour

- 90 minutes

- 2 hours or more

These are categories that Amazon will put you in if they think your page length falls within it. Western Shorts, the highly coveted, drool-worthy category many of my author friends and I long to be in, is also one. It has dedicated fans who browse specifically for short western romances—making it easier to reach our ideal readers. You'll find you have certain categories as well you want to be in, and learn how to best get there the more you write.

As a reminder, I'd said in Chapter 1 the how you get there is a mystery, and things change. Watch your book's categories over the course of a week. It may change, even though you did nothing. While we have some control over this, we don't have exact control, which is why your keywords are so critical to get right.

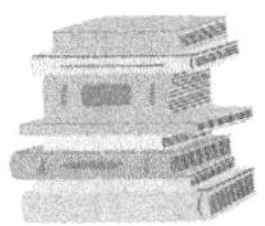

MARKETING YOUR BOOK ON THE CHEAP

You've written your heart out, edited carefully, and gotten a gorgeous cover. But nobody's buying. Sound familiar? Don't panic—your book probably just needs some strategic marketing.

Now, no need to worry! I'm not talking about spending hundreds. Hence, the title of this chapter. While you can spend your money on advertisements, that might not be something you want to do right away. You may want to wait until you have a few books under your belt to maximize those ads. Your marketing decisions are completely your own, but I want to share a few of the ways you might not have realized that you could utilize to get the word out about your book, and get new eyes on it.

Here are some of the most effective free and low-cost marketing strategies for romance authors. Pick a few that feel natural to you—you don't need to do them all at once!

- Social media

- Newsletters

- Cross promotions

- ARC readers

- Reader magnets

- Paid promos/Giveaways

- Sites like BookBub/Goodreads

- Amazon Author Central

- Book tours/Guest blog posts

- YouTube/Podcasts

- Keeping your backlist active

Unfamiliar with how to use these? Let me explain a little.

Social media

Social media is likely one of the most common ways to share about your book. No matter what platform you use, there will be readers there. Your posts, videos, and networking or dropping in to share a new release is going to get eyes on your book.

What are some ways that you can leverage social media to share about your books?

- Post about your new releases.

- Make games with your new releases, like word searches, jigsaw puzzles, or predictive text.

- Seek groups where you can share your new release. Ones that are active and not spammy are the best bets to actually get readers.

- Cross-promote with other authors. Offer to share their title on your socials if they'll share yours.

- Find (or ask about) author parties or takeovers or posting events. They are fantastic for getting readers excited about your books and also get your name in front of similar authors for future invitations to their events.

- Do a virtual launch party. It doesn't have to be huge, it doesn't have to be crazy. It could be as simple as you doing a post a day for a week, with games, short videos of you reading, whatever. Just something to make them want to come back the next day and see what you are doing.

Romance readers are particularly active on Facebook, Instagram, TikTok, and Pinterest. Choose one or two platforms to focus on rather than spreading yourself too thin. Something that I personally like to do is add one new thing a quarter to how I run my business. Then, I'm not feeling overwhelmed with trying to do all of the things in all of the places.

Newsletters

Everyone talks about a newsletter. Do you know why? Building a newsletter is important. If you were to get locked out of your socials or have an issue with your account, how would you let everyone know?

A newsletter lets you share with your readers all the good stuff about you at once. Your new releases, sales, updates, whatever. You can use one for further cross promotions as well, by joining a newsletter swap on Facebook or through a site like BookFunnel or StoryOrigin. After all, your 1,000 or 2,000 or 5,000 newsletter subs might not be the same as mine.

Popular newsletter platforms include MailChimp, MailerLite, and ConvertKit. BookFunnel and StoryOrigin also offer newsletter tools specifically for authors. Some of these newsletter platforms don't even charge you if your newsletter subscription list is under 1,000.

While it can take a little while to build your newsletter subscriber list, it will never grow if you don't work on it. It's okay to start small; we all started with zero, but be consistent in your sending. Once a month, twice a month, whatever. Set your days and send. Consider giving a reader magnet to encourage signups for your newsletter growth, like a bonus story that's exclusive for your newsletter subscribers or a bonus epilogue.

Additionally, there are newsletter builder promos you can join. I've been in some for as little as twenty-five dollars that added hundreds of subscribers (who stuck around!) to my newsletter list. These promos work by offering a giveaway to readers, and to enter, they must sign up for your newsletter. When you have ten or twenty authors in a similar genre to you sharing about the giveaway, you not only get new readers but also ones who are already reading the kinds of books you write!

Reader Magnets

If I lost you when I mentioned reader magnets, let me go a little more in depth about those. A reader magnet is a gift. It's a free sample of your writing. For the new-to-you reader, it's a chance to see if they like what you write and how you write it. For existing readers, it's a bonus little glimpse into the world you've created.

There are a few types of reader magnets. Some are a bonus epilogue or bonus scene. Those are quick and easy to write. Others are a full-sized story or novella. You could also do an audiobook, or a collection of recipes, or even a playlist.

It doesn't really matter what you do for your reader magnet, but you want it to be something the reader will find value in, and enjoy. After all, if they are giving you their email address in trade for you writing them a few times a month, they need to feel that they also got something from you.

Stuff Your Kindle Days

There are a few events, both those largely organized and those that are smaller, where authors come together to offer their book for free or .99 for a single day. There is so much power in that cross promotion. The first one I joined had over 500 participating authors, and each of us promoted the event to our newsletter lists.

I was shocked that I had over 2,000 downloads on my title. I also gained a ton of reviews and from that point on, my royalties went from double digits to triple digits each month, and have just continued up. A recent promo had well over 1,500 authors. My book got far more exposure than it would have had I just dropped it to free and shared to my current readers.

The best promos like this will be the ones where your readers are. It's 100% okay (in my opinion) to join a promotion in romance where there are mixed heat levels or subgenres, meaning that there might be mysteries and fantasy along with the romances. I always warn my readers to check before one-clicking if they only want clean books or just romance, but I've also never been in one where there wasn't a designated "clean" category or a category that divided the books by subgenre.

ARC Readers

An ARC reader is short for an Advance Copy Reader. These are readers who get your eBook for free from you, in hopes that they'll leave a review or share about it on socials. Amazon's terms of service prohibit offering payment or incentives for reviews, and you can't demand reviews or require them to be positive. However, providing free ARCs and asking for honest reviews is perfectly acceptable and industry standard. Those early-days reviews often make the difference between a book getting some notice, or taking a long time to gain traction.

While the numbers will fluctuate as to how many reviews you get, it's been my personal experience that at least 50% of the ARC copies I send out get a review. How many copies you want to send out is up to you. I send around twenty-five, sometimes as many as thirty-five. An author acquaintance sends a few hundred. In her opinion, she can't send too many. I tend to be conservative. Find what works for you, and hopefully that review, plus their social media shout-out, gains you new readers.

You can find ARC readers through word of mouth. There are also several Facebook groups for seeking them. One of the easiest ways to collect names for your ARC team is to create a Google form, so that you can get their name, email address, and anything else you'd want to know, like the name they use to post under.

The majority of authors (myself included) use eBooks for their ARCs. There will always be readers who say they only read physical copies. Those can be very expensive to send out, and there's no guarantee that they will review. I prefer to use physical copies as giveaway prizes for readers. However, the choice is a personal one to make.

A last word on ARC readers or readers in general. Don't let yourself be guilted into anything, especially making book donations. It's very easy for that to happen, and it's happened to me a few times where I gave away eBook or paperback copies to people who sounded legitimate and turned out not to be or who never sent a thank you after a donation or followed through with a tax receipt. If you are writing in part to pay bills, you've got to find that fine line between being reader generous and being business savvy.

Paid Promos/Giveaways/Builders

There are many paid promo opportunities out there that don't cost a lot. Everything from newsletter builders where you pay a small fee that goes into a large giveaway prize while also getting new subscribers for your newsletter, to paid spots for your book to be featured in a newsletter that goes out to tens of thousands of subscribers.

For many of the newsletter builders, the premise is the same as your standard cross promotion. All authors involved are sharing the giveaway, and gaining new subscribers from the pool of similar authors who these readers weren't aware of. Some of these even have add-ons available, where you can collect followers on your Amazon page, any social pages, or BookBub.

Research promo sites that specialize in your genre and read reviews from other authors who write books similar to what you do before spending money.

BookBub

At the time of writing this, it's totally free to join BookBub and get an author profile. Hopefully, that never changes. This is a fantastic and FREE tool for marketing because BookBub does a few pretty nice things for authors.

First, it sends out new release alerts! That's right. When you add a book to BookBub, it lets anyone who is following you know that it's your release day! Second, it also lets readers follow you and recommend your book. That's a great thing, because when someone new finds you, they can see your book has been recommended. BookBub offers other things as well, but those two are totally free, and should be part of your marketing plan.

Occasionally, I like to post on my socials that people can follow me on BookBub. You never know who will want to sign up and follow, and potentially forward an email to a friend sharing about your new release they enjoyed.

Goodreads

Many authors like using Goodreads. There's no cost to create an author profile, and they offer services for authors like giveaways. Their forum can be a good place to interact with authors and author service providers, and of course, it's a way to help promote your books or gain followers. That said, since in those forums those are individuals, not a company, be careful, just the same as you would be with anyone else approaching you for a service.

Amazon Author Central

It's crazy to me the number of authors who write their books and have them on KDP, but don't make their author profile. That, my friends, is a wasted opportunity. You can have a little "about me" area, encourage people to follow you, and when you've got a new release, Amazon will email them! You might even find your book recommended in an email. Why wouldn't you want to do that?

I can't tell you the number of times I've clicked on an author's name under a book I thought sounded interesting to see what else they've written, and it didn't take me to their author profile, just a search page with books that were not even theirs. That's such a missed chance for reader-author connection and sales.

It doesn't take long to set your profile up, and it's a fantastic tool to use. Anything that reminds readers you have an upcoming release and also that doesn't cost you anything is a great marketing tool.

Blog Tours and Guest Posting

Blog tours involve your book being featured across multiple blogs over several days or weeks, with reviews, interviews, or guest posts. Prices vary, and effectiveness depends on the blogs' readership. Guest blog posts are often free—you write an article for a book blog in exchange for exposure to their audience. Sometimes you might be asked to provide a giveaway.

While blog tours are found usually through searching online, the guest posts are often word of mouth or a sign-up dropped in a Facebook group or reading community. Keep your eyes open, and if you miss one, don't be afraid to ask when the next will be so you can join.

YouTube Channel/Podcast

It's not hard at all to start your own YouTube channel. You could do one talking about the writing journey, or you could do one and read from your book or share about it. I have one simply to drop my book trailers I create so I have an URL to share them, and it's there waiting for when I decide to grow it more.

Podcasts are also a popular way to get in front of others. Look for those hosted by authors in your subgenre or when you see someone post.

I've been invited to a few, simply by seeing another author say: Hey! I've got open spots. Anyone want to join in? Your readers will enjoy getting to see you, and you might make some connections with other authors to open doors for cross promotion.

Keeping Your Backlist Active

It's a fact that the books we've released don't stay as popular. Sales drop off. But it doesn't have to be that way. Keep your backlist in the spotlight by continuing to promote them. For example, every Friday, I share an excerpt from a backlist book. I keep those older titles in BookFunnel promos. Several times a year, I'll drop one to .99, and do a paid promo on it.

I have found that by doing so, any books that are linked to that title, by character, town, or theme, have a small uptick afterward. Keeping your backlist active by promotion of single titles or creating a box set lets the hard work you've done in creating your book continue to make you money and get you new readers. There is very little effort required, but the payoff could be huge.

This is just the tip of the iceberg when it comes to free or cheap promotions. Did any of these spark some ideas? There's one more I'm going to mention in the final chapter, and it's all about multi-author collabs. Ready for the wrap-up?

Now What?

You did it. You wrote your book, and it's ready to go into the world. Now what? Here is what I suggest.

- Seek out others who write similarly to you

- Keep writing

- Be patient

- Don't give up if it takes time to grow your readership

I wish I could shout that last one. Can you just pretend I did? Maybe with a pleading look in my eyes as I grab your shoulders and do a little dramatic shaking? This is so important.

Just like with anything we do in life, we don't (usually) get instant results of success. Did you drive perfectly the first time? Cook a meal perfectly? Spell a really complicated word? Of course not! But if you stop because of fear of failure, you for sure aren't going to get to where you want to go.

Most authors don't see significant income until they have multiple books published. Your first book is practice. Your tenth book benefits from nine others supporting it with also-boughts and read-through.

Ensure you maintain your momentum. Continue marketing your book after the launch with the places I mentioned in the previous chapter. Engage with your readers. Even if you don't have many, we all start with zero, so don't feel less than any other author if that's where you are. It takes time to grow anything, including your readership.

Here are some ways to do that.

- Respond to comments and messages left on your socials or emailed

- Ask questions in your newsletter and reply to answers, even if it's just a thank you or telling someone to have a good weekend

- Create a reader group and post regularly

- Thank reviewers (without being pushy about it)

- Do more interactive posts than sales posts

Above all, don't let slow growth discourage you. Keep talking to your newsletter as though you don't just have five subs. Be consistent in what you do, and it will grow. I promise you that. In this genre, cross promotion is often what gets your foot in the door, so to speak.

When it comes to continuing to write, figure out your plan. How quickly you publish is up to you and your life circumstances. Some authors release weekly, others monthly, others quarterly. Find a sustainable pace—burnout helps no one. Consistency matters more than speed.

Are you interested in just writing standalone titles? Do you want to do a series? Do you want the best of both worlds for a time, so the weight of all the promotion isn't fully on your shoulders?

If the answer to that third question is YES, then seek out multi-author collabs or multi-author projects (MAPS). This is a collaborative series where multiple authors each write their own book around a shared theme. Think snowed in at Christmas, mail-order husband, vacation romance. Each of these authors write and upload their own book, but everyone shares about everyone else's release, and it cross promotes, helping you to pool your readers and grow collectively.

You can find these collabs through Facebook groups and author friends. If you suddenly see several authors all promoting books with similar covers or in the same series, reach out and ask how you can get involved with a future project. They can usually point you to the person who led that one.

When in a multi-author project, look for active organizers, ones who have run successful series before and have both a good reputation and good follow-through. Seek ones with clear guidelines, those willing to help you get your feet wet, and compatible heat levels or subgenres to what you currently write or want to write.

Some collabs don't require a financial contribution (called a buy in), and all of the expenses you incur, such as for your cover, are your own, but others do—typically $100–$200+ to cover your share of cover design, advertising, and other promotional expenses. Be sure to ask what is included, and if possible, talk to other authors who have worked with this leader before to see how they felt previous experiences went.

However, sharing confidential information about the series—themes, covers, or marketing plans—outside the collab group before the official reveal is a huge no-no and will get you passed over for future opportunities.

Some red flags to look for (that you might only recognize after being in a few multi-author projects) are leaders who are disorganized, lack of promotion from other authors (or promotion only for a few select authors), too many books in the series, or unclear expectations.

While these projects can be fun and really get your name out there, you want to be careful you are with the right group, one who will support you and help you meet your author goals.

Above all else, don't let others you meet on your writing journey demotivate you. You'll encounter discouragement—sometimes from jealous competitors, sometimes from well-meaning people who don't understand publishing. Focus on your goals and supportive writing friends, not the negativity.

Writing is hard. Marketing is hard. Putting yourself out there is hard. But the reward of holding your book in your hands, hearing a reader talk about how much they loved it...that makes it all worthwhile.

You are down to the final few pages. You've learned how to craft compelling characters, create emotional stakes, write clean heat, and get your book into readers' hands. That's huge! Not everyone finishes a book. Not everyone publishes. But you? You're doing it. I'm proud of you, and I can't wait to see what you write next. Stay motivated, and keep going. You're going to find the resources on the next page. But first? One last piece of writing advice.

Don't give up. You've got this.

RESOURCES

Now it's time for all the lists! From trope lists to pre-writing and post-writing checklists, these next pages are all of that important information. Want a FREE twenty-eight page downloadable and printable list of these lists and checklists? No problem! I created one just for you. All I ask is that you don't copy the pages or claim them as your own. If you'd like to share with someone else, give them the URL. You can find the downloadable after the section called Bonus: Red Flags.

And now, here are the lists.

ROMANCE TROPES LIST

While not an all-inclusive list, I've got quite a few here for you to mix and match. Remember to be realistic with the tropes you use. Don't put a trope in just for the sake of having one, but do use them in a strategic way that makes your story better.

1. **Enemies to Lovers** - Characters who start off disliking each other but then fall in love

2. **Friends to Lovers** - Two friends realize that their feelings run deeper

3. **Fake Dating/Relationship** - Pretending to be together leads to real feelings

4. **Second Chance Romance** - Rekindling a relationship that hadn't worked out or else a character(s) who previously had a failed relationship find love

5. **Forced Proximity** - Stuck together in close quarters (think elevator, car, locked room)

6. **Grumpy/Sunshine** - A cynic or moody person, and one who is always cheerful and optimistic

7. **One Bed** - With only one bed, what will happen?

8. **Love Triangle** - One character is torn between two love interests

9. **Forbidden Love** - A relationship that breaks rules or societal expectations

10. **Secret Relationship** - Hiding their romance from others. Could easily be paired with Forbidden Love

11. **Marriage of Convenience** - Characters marrying for practical reasons, and not love (at first)

12. **Arranged Marriage** - There was no say in the marriage for the characters

13. **Boss/Employee/Coworker**   -   Workplace romance, and works well when there's a power dynamic

14. **Bodyguard Romance** - Falls for the person they're guarding/Falls for the person guarding them.

15. **Royalty Romance** - Falling for a prince, princess, duke, duchess, etc.

16. **Small Town Romance** - Finding love in a small town (Pairs well with second chance tropes)

17. **Billionaire Romance** - Wealthy love interest sweeps them off their feet. Billionaire might be a jerk or might be a sweet person

18. **Age Gap** - One character is older than the other, which leads to conflicts

19. **Childhood Sweetheart** - Can either be an always known they'd be together or else reconnecting

20. **Opposites Attract** - Very different people fall for each other, like a billionaire and a struggling waitress.

21. **Unrequited Love** - A one-sided love that eventually becomes mutual

22. **Amnesia** - Memory loss affects the relationship or even creates it

23. **Mistaken Identity** - Someone is confused for someone else and they play along

24. **Reformed** - A known heartbreaker settles down...or do they?

25. **Fish Out of Water** - Character(s) in an unfamiliar situation

26. **Protégé/Mentor Romance** - Student falls for teacher or guide or vice versa

27. **Star-Crossed Lovers** - Fate seems to work against them, every single time

28. **Rescue Romance** - A rescue by one leads to love

29. **Secret Baby** - One person didn't know about their child

30. **Brother's/Sister's Best Friend** - Falling for a sibling's friend

31. **Best Friend's Sibling** - Falling for friend's

brother or sister

32. **Snowed In/Trapped Together** - Weather or circumstances force proximity in a situation where there isn't an immediate escape

33. **Nanny/Babysitter** - A child's caregiver falls for employer or vice versa

34. **Cowboy Romance** - Western setting

35. **Sports** - Athlete(s) finds love. May or may not be between fan or non-athlete.

36. **Vacation** - Falling in love with someone while on vacation

37. **Christmas** - A romance that takes place during Christmas

38. **Roommates** - Living together leads to love

39. **Soulmate/Fated Mates** - Characters are destined to be together

40. **Revenge Romance** - Initially, one is motivated by vengeance, not love

41. **Beauty and the Beast** - One partner is an outcast

42. **Cinderella** - Rags to riches because of the romance

43. **Accidental Pregnancy** - An unexpected baby brings them together

44. **Mistaken for a Couple** - Others assume they're dating, so they go for it and it turns real

45. **Pen Pals/Long Distance** - Falling in love from afar; can be through letters, text, etc.

46. **Single Parent Romance** - Finding love while raising a child solo

47. **Stranded Together** - Stuck on an island, in the wilderness, etc.

48. **Secret Identity** - One partner is hiding who they really are from the other

49. **Widow/Widower Romance** - Finding love after loss

50. **Matchmaker** - A third party brings together the couple

51. **Sworn Off Love** - Character(s) vowed never to love again

52. **Love Potion/Spell** - Magic influences feelings, but then becomes real

53. **Neighbor Romance** - Falling in love with the one next door

54. **Unpopular/Popular** - Different social circles, yet feelings arise

55. **Accidental Kiss** - A mistaken kiss sparks feelings

56. **Bet/Dare Romance** - What started as a game becomes real

57. **Marriage Pact** - Friends agree to marry if still single by certain age

58. **Celebrity Romance** - A famous person falls for a regular person, or else a regular person gets a chance to be with a celebrity.

59. **Sworn Enemies** - Feuding families, or those who used to be friends

60. **Lost** - Losing their way might be the best thing to ever happen to them

LIST OF SETTINGS FOR YOUR SCENES

Feeling stuck about where you should put your couple? Here is a list of some settings that you might not have thought of.

1. **Remote lighthouse**

2. **Carnival**

3. **Bustling subway station**

4. **Historical site**

5. **Volunteer spot**

6. **Library**

7. **Small-town diner**

8. **Destination vacation**

9. **Art gallery or museum**

10. **Military base**

11. **Snowy mountain cabin**

12. **In the woods**

13. **Workplace**

14. **Hospital emergency room**

15. **Friend/Family's home**

16. **Club/bar**

17. **Store**

18. **Prison**

19. **Dusty antique shop**

20. **Vineyard**

21. **Church**

22. **School**

23. **Rooftop garden**

24. **Veterinary clinic**

25. **Train**

26. **Archaeological dig site**

27. **Cattle ranch**

28. **Horse farm**

29. **Hot air balloon**

30. **Beach**

31. **Airport**

32. **Concert**

33. **Local park**

34. **Grocery store**

35. **Repair shop**

36. **Fishing spot**

37. **Lake/Ocean/Stream/Pond**

38. **Café**

39. **Bookshop**

40. **Gas station**

41. **Ghost town**

42. **Restaurant**

43. **Convention**

44. **Movie theater**

45. **Theatre**

46. **Government building**

47. **Hedge maze/Corn maze**

48. **Port harbor**

49. **Laundromat**

50. **Arcade**

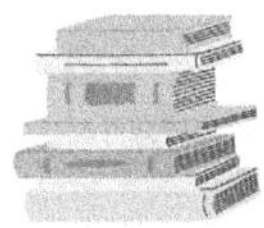

Internal and External Conflict Starter List

Remember, an internal conflict is one that's happening inside of your character. An external conflict is one that's happening to them. Here's a list for you to spark some ideas for your bite-sized stories.

Internal Conflicts

1. **Fear of Abandonment**

2. **Unworthiness**

3. **It's Too Good to Be True**

4. **Survivor's Guilt**

5. **Need for Perfectionism**

6. **Secret Dream**

7. **Fear of Losing Something**

8. **Feels Love Would be Irresponsible**

9. **Mistrust**

10. **Unfinished Goal**

11. **Past Trauma**

12. **Feels Second Best**

13. **Lack of Trust**

14. **Lonely**

15. **Fear of Vulnerability**

16. **Feels Judged**

17. **Afraid of Happiness**

18. **Conflicting Situation/Personality**

19. **Self-Doubt**

20. **Secret Burden**

21. **Need to Prove Themselves**

22. **Idealization versus Reality**

23. **Likes to be Alone**

24. **Weight of an Obligation**

25. **Fear of Intimacy (Non-physical or physical)**

26. **Feels Betrayed**

27. **Unwilling to Forgive**

28. **Pressure**

29. **Conflicting Morals**

30. **Past Failures**

External Conflicts

1. **Logistical Problems**

2. **Rival Companies**

3. **Family Intervention**

4. **Forced Proximity**

5. **Secret Identity**

6. **Single Parent**

7. **Misinterpreted Gesture**

8. **Language Barrier**

9. **Financial Situation**

10. **Falsely Accused**

11. **Natural Disaster/Severe Weather**

12. **Personality Clash**

13. **Cultural/Upbringing Differences**

14. **Dependent Family Member**

15. **Time Limit**

16. **Mistaken Identity**

17. **Addiction**

18. **Immoral Behavior**

19. **Ethical Dilemma**

20. **Loss of Property**

BOOK READINESS CHECKLISTS

Before You Write Checklist

Story Planning

- Choose your word count goal (short story: 1,000–7,500 | novelette: 7,500–17,500 | novella: 17,500–40,000)

- Select your trope(s) (refer to the trope list in this book for some ideas)

- Decide on your setting (refer to the setting list to jump-start your ideas)

- Determine your heat level (kisses only, closed door, etc.)

- Plan your main characters' desires, fears, and emotional wounds

- Identify internal and external conflicts

- Know your ending (HEA or HFN)

WRITING YOUR STORY CHECKLIST

Essential Story Elements

- Create believable main characters with depth

- Establish supporting characters (if word count allows)

- Open with a strong hook that establishes mood and character

- Include a memorable meet-cute (within first 10–15% of story)

- Build emotional stakes throughout

- Use internal dialogue/monologue to reveal character thoughts

- Show, don't tell (except for time jumps and backstory)

- Create sensory details and vivid settings

- Layer in your chosen trope(s) naturally

- Build to the "all is lost" moment (around 75% mark)

- Include a grand gesture and resolution

- End with a satisfying HEA or HFN with a promise of forever

CLEAN ROMANCE SPECIFICS

- Build physical tension through non-sexual sensory details (scent, sound, touch, proximity)

- Make every touch meaningful and progressive

- Use emotional connection to replace physical intimacy

- Create chemistry through dialogue and longing looks

- Include moments of distraction/interruption to build tension

SELF-EDITING CHECKLIST

The Waiting Period

- Set manuscript aside for at least 2–3 days (ideally 1–2 weeks)

- Work on your next project during this time

Self-Editing Tasks

- Read-through for major story issues (plot holes, timeline problems)

- Check character name consistency

- Verify that character traits/descriptions remain consistent

- Remove redundant words and filter words

- Replace weak verbs with stronger ones

- Eliminate unnecessary telling (replace with showing where important)

- Add sensory details where scenes feel flat

- Ensure dialogue sounds natural and character-specific

- Check that conflict escalates properly

- Verify the resolution feels earned

Technical Self-Edit

- Run spell check

- Read aloud or use text-to-speech to catch errors

- Print manuscript and read on paper (optional but helpful)

- Check for:

- Missing or incorrect punctuation

- Dialogue formatting

- Paragraph breaks

- Scene transitions

- Chapter consistency

BETA READERS AND PROFESSIONAL EDITING CHECKLIST

Beta Readers (Optional but Recommended)

- Send to 3–5 beta readers

- Ask specific questions about plot, characters, pacing

- Give them 1–2 weeks to read and respond

- Compile feedback and decide what resonates

- Make revisions based on beta feedback

Professional Editing

- Decide which type of edit you need:

  - Developmental edit (if struggling with plot/structure)

  - Copy/line edit (if story works but needs polishing)

  - Hybrid edit (combination of both)

  - Proofread (final polish before publication)

- Research and contact editors (get sample edits, compare rates)

- Book your edit

- Provide a clean manuscript to your editor

- Review edits carefully and address any queries

- Make final revisions

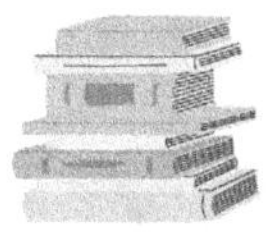

PREPARING TO PUBLISH CHECKLIST

After Editing

- Do one final proofread yourself

- Consider hiring a proofreader for final pass

- Ensure all edits are incorporated and nothing went wonky during revisions

Front and Back Matter

- Create title page

- Write copyright page (include editor or cover designer credit if required by contract)

- Add dedication (optional)

- Create table of contents

- Write author bio

- Add social media links and website

- List other books (if applicable)

- Include newsletter signup information

- Add sneak peek of next book (optional)

ISBN/ASIN

- Decide if you'll use free ASIN from platform or purchase ISBN

- If buying ISBN, purchase from Bowker (US) or your country's agency

- Get separate ISBN/ASIN for each format (eBook, paperback, hardcover, audiobook)

Book Description/Blurb

- Write compelling book description for retailer pages

- Include tropes/hooks that will attract your readers

- Keep it concise (150–250 words)

- End with a question or teaser

- Save this for your cover designer (needed for paperback back cover)

FORMATTING CHECKLIST

Choose Your Formatting Method

- DIY in Word

- Use formatting software (Vellum, Atticus, Draft2Digital, etc.)

- Hire a professional formatter

eBook Formatting

- Ensure clickable table of contents

- Check that chapter headings are consistent

- Verify all links work (to other books, newsletter, social media)

- Test on multiple devices if possible

- Create file in required format (ePub, Word doc, etc.)

Paperback Formatting (if applicable)

- Choose trim size (5x8, 6x9, etc.)

- Set correct margins and gutters

- Ensure proper bleed settings

- Include page numbers (not on title page or chapter starts, typically)

- Start chapters on right-hand pages

- Create PDF file for printer

- Note page count (needed for cover)

- Note paper type choice: cream or white (affects spine width)

Cover Design Checklist

Before Contacting Designer

- Browse covers in your subgenre to understand expectations

- Save 3–5 comparison covers you like

- Prepare book description/blurb

- Decide which formats you need (eBook, paperback, hardcover, audiobook)

- For paperback: have trim size, page count, and paper type ready

Working with Designer

- Research cover designers (Fiverr, Etsy, Upwork, word of mouth)

- Review their portfolio

- Request quote and timeline

- Decide between custom or premade

- Provide comp titles, blurb, and any specific requests

- Be clear about what you DON'T want

- Review design at thumbnail size

- Request revisions if needed (typically 2–3 rounds included)

- Get final files in all required formats and sizes

Cover Checklist

- Title is readable at thumbnail size

- Cover is on-brand for your subgenre

- Colors and style match genre expectations

- No spelling errors on cover

- Author name is correct and legible

- Back cover has blurb, author bio, barcode space (paperback)

- Spine text is correct and properly sized (paperback)

Uploading and Pre-Launch Checklist

- Create accounts on chosen platforms (Amazon KDP, Draft2Digital, etc.)

- Upload manuscript file

- Upload cover file

- Fill in book details:

  - Title, subtitle, author name

- Book description

- Keywords

- Categories

- Age range/content ratings if required

- Set pricing

- Choose distribution options (KU exclusive or wide)

- Set pre-order date (optional)

- Preview book carefully before approving

- Order proof copy (paperback) to check before approval

Pre-Launch Tasks

- Set up book on BookBub (free author profile)

- Add book to Goodreads

- Add book to Amazon Author Central

- Create social media graphics

- Write social media posts for launch week

- Prepare newsletter announcement

- Recruit ARC readers (2–4 weeks before launch)

- Send ARC copies with polite review request

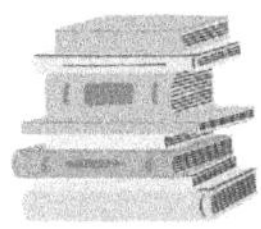

LAUNCH DAY MARKETING CHECKLIST

- Publish or ensure pre-order goes live

- Post on all social media platforms

- Send newsletter to subscribers

- Update website/blog

- Thank ARC readers

- Engage with comments and messages

- Consider a virtual launch party or week-long event

First Week After Launch

- Continue posting about book on social media

- Join "new release" promo groups on Facebook

- Cross-promote with other authors

- Monitor for reviews and thank reviewers (without being pushy)

- Track sales and read-through to other books

- Adjust keywords/categories if needed based on performance

ONGOING MARKETING CHECKLIST

- Post regularly on social media (more interaction than sales posts)

- Build your newsletter list consistently

- Participate in newsletter swaps

- Join Stuff Your Kindle or similar multi-author promos

- Continue recruiting and sending to ARC readers

- Maintain BookBub and Goodreads presence

- Keep Amazon Author Central updated

- Look for blog tour and guest post opportunities

- Consider starting a YouTube channel or podcast

- Seek multi-author collab opportunities

Paid Marketing (when ready)

- Research promo sites (Robin Reads, Fussy Librarian, etc.)

- Try newsletter builder giveaways

- Apply for BookBub Featured Deals

- Test Facebook/Amazon ads (once you have multiple books)

WHAT NEXT? CHECKLIST

Building Your Backlist

- Start your next book

- Maintain a consistent release schedule (weekly, monthly, or quarterly)

- Write in series when possible (or connected standalones)

- Cross-promote all your books in back matter

- Update older books' back matter as you release new titles

- Don't give up! Remember, most authors need several books to see significant income

Community

- Connect with other clean romance authors

- Join supportive Facebook groups

- Engage with readers authentically

- Focus on supportive relationships, not competition

- Keep learning and improving your craft

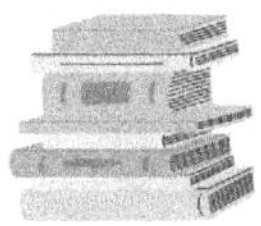

BONUS: RED FLAGS TO AVOID

Don't:

- Upload your first draft without self-editing

- Skip editing entirely

- Use unlicensed images or make your own cover without proper tools

- Choose an off-brand cover to "stand out"

- Ignore formatting (readers notice!)

- Spam reader groups with constant book promotions

- Offer incentives for reviews (against Amazon TOS)

- Give up after one book

- Compare your beginning to someone else's middle

- Let jealous or negative people derail you

Remember: Every published author started exactly where you are now. Take it one step at a time, do your best work, and keep moving forward. You've got this!

DON'T FORGET!

You can get your downloadable twenty-eight page copy of these lists and checklists here: https://dl.bookfunnel.com/7dbo8697eu

Note from Author

Thank you for taking the time to read *Bite-Sized Romance*. Could I ask for one small favor? Reviews like yours on Amazon mean so much to me and help others to find my books! Even just a single line means a lot!

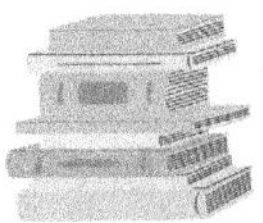

ABOUT THE AUTHOR

Sarah writes captivating characters and clean romance that's anything BUT boring! From heartbreaking moments to heartwarming tales, get swept away in either historical or small town romance that pulls you in until the last page.

Nestled in the Blue Ridge Mountains of Virginia where she's married to her Texan husband, you'll find Sarah creating her next book, spending time with her children, or volunteering in her community.

Want more of Sarah's books? Find them all on Amazon!

https://www.amazon.com/stores/Sarah-Lamb/author/B098H3SGLK

9 781960 418654